Blooming Crochet Hats

10 Crochet Designs with 10 Mix-and-Match Accents

Shauna-Lee Graham
of Bouquet Beanies

CINCINNATI, OHIO

Table of Contents

Introduction

I remember the day in September 2009 when I was contacted by two photographers who wanted me to design hats with flowers on them for their photo shoots. As I was sewing the flowers onto the hats, it hit me! Why was I making the hat so final when I could just add a button to it? Then the wearer could interchange the flowers to create a true masterpiece perfect for any occasion. At that moment, Bouquet Beanies was born!

I love to create new styles and designs. I feel a sense of accomplishment when I complete a new pattern. They are like my children—unique and beautiful in their own way, and I'm so excited to share them all with you!

Enjoy, have fun and let your creativity shine!

Shauna

Stitches & Techniques

Learn to Crochet

The stitches illustrated below will be used throughout the book. Use this guide if you aren't certain what to do or what a particular abbreviation means.

Slip Knot *(diag. 1)*

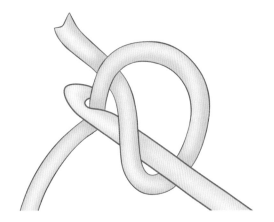

Form a loop, put the hook in the loop and draw another loop through.

Slip Knot *(diag. 2)*

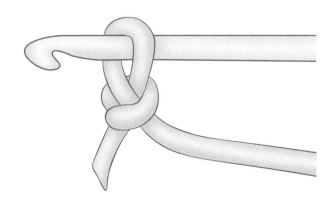

Slide the knot up the hook and tighten gently.

Chain (ch)

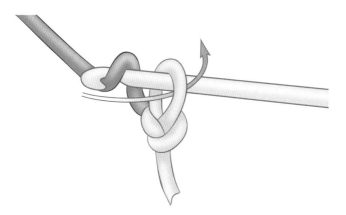

With the hook through the slip knot, yarn over hook (yoh) and pull the yarn through the loop to make a new chain (ch). Chain stitch (ch st) made.

Forming a Ring

Chain (ch) as many stitches as indicated, insert the hook in the 1st ch, yarn over hook (yoh) and pull through the 1st ch and the ch on the hook.

Single Crochet (sc) *(diag. 1)*

Insert the hook into the 2nd chain (ch) from the hook, yarn over hook (yoh) and draw the yarn through the work only.

Single Crochet (sc) *(diag. 2)*

Yoh again and draw through both loops on the hook. Single crochet (sc) made. Repeat as indicated.

Half Double Crochet (hdc)

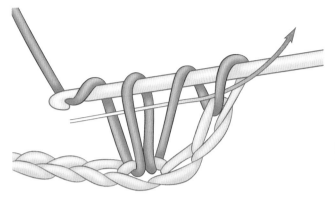

Yarn over hook (yoh), insert the hook into the 3rd chain (ch) from the hook, yoh and draw through the work only, yoh and draw through all 3 loops on the hook. Half double crochet (hdc) made. Repeat as indicated.

Double Crochet (dc) *(diag. 1)*

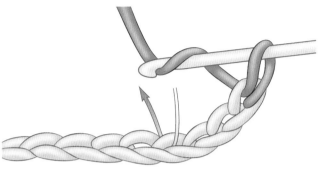

Yarn over hook (yoh) and insert the hook into the 4th chain (ch) from the hook.

Double Crochet (dc) *(diag. 2)*

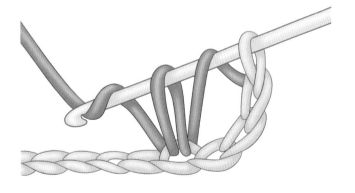

Yoh, draw through the work only, yoh and draw through the first 2 loops on the hook.

Double Crochet (dc) *(diag. 3)*

Yoh and draw through the remaining 2 loops on the hook. Double crochet (dc) made. Repeat as indicated.

Treble Crochet (tc) *(diag. 1)*

Yarn over hook (yoh) twice, insert the hook into the 5th chain (ch) from the hook and draw up a loop.

Treble Crochet (tc) *(diag. 2)*

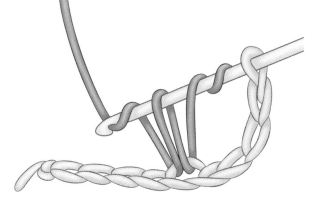

Yoh and draw through the 2 loops on the hook.

Treble Crochet (tc) *(diag. 3)*

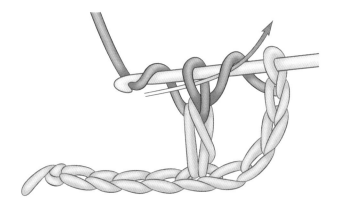

Yoh and draw through the next 2 loops on the hook.

Treble Crochet (tc) *(diag. 4)*

Yoh and draw through the last 2 loops on the hook. Treble crochet (tc) made. Repeat as indicated.

Slip Stitch (sl st)

Insert the hook into the 2nd chain (ch) from the hook. Yarn over hook (yoh) and draw the yarn through both the work and the loop on the hook at the same time. Slip stitch (sl st) made.

Front Loop (flp) / Back Loop (blp)

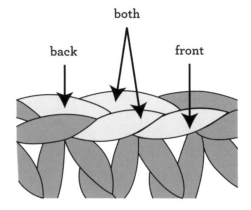

both

back

front

Working in the front loop (flp) or back loop (blp) as directed in the pattern.

Front Post Double Crochet (fpdc)

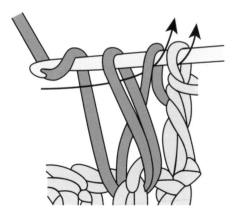

Yarn over hook (yoh), insert the hook from the front to the back around the stitch (post) of the previous row, draw up a loop, yoh, draw through the 2 loops on the hook, yoh and draw through the last 2 loops on the hook.

Back Post Double Crochet (bpdc)

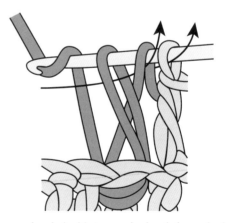

Yarn over hook (yoh), insert the hook from the back to the front around the stitch (post) of the previous row, draw up a loop, yoh, draw through the 2 loops on the hook, yoh and draw through the last 2 loops on the hook.

Changing Colors (CC) in Double Crochet (dc) *(diag. 1)*

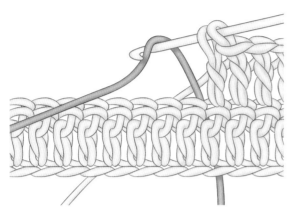

Proceed with a double crochet (dc) stitch until 2 loops remain on the hook, then draw the new color of yarn through.

Changing Colors (CC) in Double Crochet (dc) *(diag. 2)*

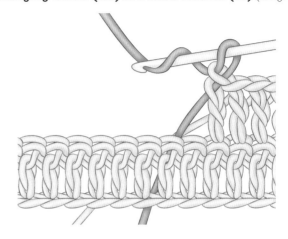

Yarn over hook (yoh).

Changing Colors (CC) in Double Crochet (dc) *(diag. 3)*

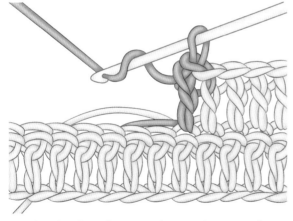

Proceed with a dc in the new color. Cut the yarn color you are not using and secure the ends behind the work.

3 Double Crochet Cluster Stitch (3dc-cl)

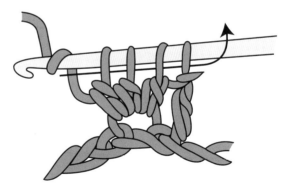

(Yarn over hook [yoh], insert the hook in the stitch indicated, draw up a loop, yoh, pull the yarn through the 2 loops on the hook) 3 times, yoh, draw through all 4 loops on the hook, yoh, draw through the loop on the hook to secure the stitch.

Puff Stitch (PS) (diag. 1)

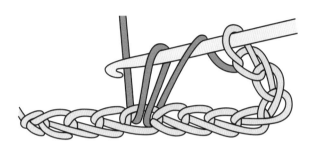

(Yarn over hook [yoh], insert the hook in the stitch and draw up a loop) 3 times.

Puff Stitch (PS) (diag. 2)

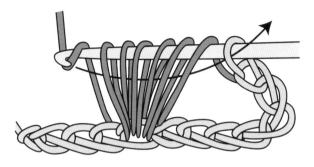

Yoh and draw through all 7 loops on the hook.

Puff Stitch (PS) (diag. 3)

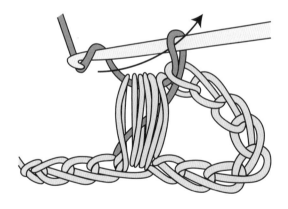

Yoh, draw though the loop on the hook to secure the stitch.

Treble Crochet V-Stitch (V-st)

(Treble crochet [tc], chain [ch] 3, tc) in the stitch indicated.

Picot Stitch *(diag. 1)*

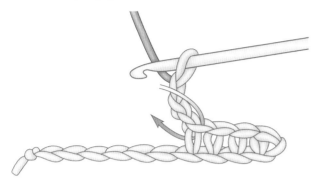

Chain (ch) 3, insert the hook through the front loop (flp) of the base stitch and left vertical bar of the base stitch.

Picot Stitch *(diag. 2)*

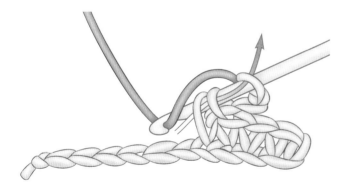

Yarn over hook (yoh) and draw through all loops on the hook.

About Buttons

We all know that young children like to put things in their mouths. They must be watched at all times while wearing items with buttons due to choking hazards. If you're concerned that your child might try to eat the buttons on the projects in this book, try one of these button alternatives. I have written two crocheted button patterns: a small one for the hats and a large one for the Twisted Headband.

Small Crochet Button Alternative

Using light sport weight yarn (3) and leaving a 7" (17.8cm) tail, ch 2.

Rnd 1: Work 8 hdc in 2nd ch from hook; join with sl st in beg hdc. (8 hdc)

Rnd 2: Ch 1, (insert hook in 1st hdc, draw up loop, insert hook in next hdc, draw up loop, yoh, draw through all 3 loops on hook) 4 times, join with a sl st to beg hdc. (4 dec made)

Fasten off.

Insert the 7" (17.8cm) yarn tail into the bottom of the button to create a filling. Using a tapestry needle, thread the other end of the yarn, gather the opening of the button, draw tight and tie.

Large Crochet Button Alternative

Using light sport weight yarn (3) and leaving a 14" (35.6cm) tail, ch 2.

Rnd 1: Work 5 hdc in 2nd ch from hook; join with sl st in beg hdc. (5 hdc)

Rnd 2: Ch 2, hdc in same st as joining, * 2 hdc in next hdc, rep from * around; join with sl st in 2nd ch of beg ch-2. (10 hdc)

Rnd 3: Ch 1, sc in same st as joining and in each st around; join with sl st in beg sc. (10 sc)

Rnd 4: Ch 1, (insert hook in 1st sc, draw up loop, insert hook in next sc, draw up loop, yoh, draw through all 3 loops on hook) 5 times; join with sl st to beg sc. (5 dec made)

Fasten off.

Insert the 14" (35.6cm) yarn tail into the bottom of the button to create a filling. Using a tapestry needle, thread the other end of the yarn, gather the opening of the button, draw tight and tie.

Glossary of Abbreviations

ch(s)	chain(s)
st(s)	stitch(s)
sl st	slip stitch
beg	beginning
rep	repeat
yoh	yarn over hook
rnd(s)	round(s)
dec	decrease
sc	single crochet
hdc	half double crochet
( )	work instructions within parentheses as many times as directed

About Skill Levels

At the beginning of each project, you'll notice a flower symbol that denotes the skill level necessary to successfully complete the project. Here is a guide for the difficulty of those levels.

 Beginner. These projects are excellent for first-time crocheters. They use basic stitches and have minimal shaping.

 Easy/Intermediate. These projects use basic stitches, repetitive stitch patterns, simple color changes and simple shaping and finishing.

Chapter 1
Hats & Hair Treasures

I've designed several hats over the years, and I have to admit, they're all my favorites. I like instant gratification when I crochet, therefore I design my patterns with quick turnaround in mind.

Nothing makes me sadder than wanting to make a pattern only to find out it's available in just one or two sizes, so my patterns include all sizes, from newborn to adult. I get so much pleasure crocheting my designs for customers, whether it's for a newborn photo shoot, family photos or everyday wear.

There are many ways to make these hats unique. Take the classic beanie. You can add a Newsboy Brim for fun, a Sunhat Brim for summer or Earflaps for the cooler months. Who wouldn't love to create her own hat to match any piece of clothing in her wardrobe? Just choose the hat design and then move on to Chapter 2 to pick a flower or motif. They interchange on the hat by simply fastening them onto the button!

Experiment using worsted weight yarn and a smaller hook to make the designs that call for sport weight yarn. This will make them thicker and warmer. You can also use two strands of sport weight yarn and a smaller hook to make the Comfy Cloche. These are just a few ways to make the designs your very own.

Scalloped Beanie

Okay, I take it back. I do have a favorite hat. It's this one. This hat is where my foray into creating interchangeable designs started. What I love about this design is that you can make it as simple or as complex as you like. Want to use a funky fiber? Do it! Have a fun, old button that needs a home? Use it!

MATERIALS

For Scalloped Beanie: Light sport weight yarn **3** in the color of your choice

- 0–3 mos. (100yd/91.4m)
- 3–6 mos. (110yd/100.6m)
- 6–12 mos. (130yd/118.9m)
- 1–3 yrs. (150yd/137.2m)
- 4–8 yrs. (160yd/146.3m)
- 9 yrs.-adult (180yd/164.6m)

For optional Newsboy Brim: Light sport weight yarn in the same color as the hat (18yd/16.5m)

For optional Sunhat Brim: Light sport weight yarn in the same color as the hat (100yd/91.4m)

Size I (5.5mm) crochet hook

⅞"–1" (2.2cm–2.5cm) button

Tapestry needle

Scissors

Finished Project Sizes

To fit approx. 0–3 months: 12"–13½" (30.5cm–34.3cm) circumference

To fit approx. 3–6 months: 14"–15" (35.6cm–38.1cm) circumference

To fit approx. 6–12 months: 15"–16½" (38.1cm–41.9cm) circumference

To fit approx. 1–3 years: 16½"–18" (41.9cm–45.7cm) circumference

To fit approx. 4–8 years: 18½"–20" (47cm–50.8cm) circumference

To fit approx. 9 years–adult: 20½"–22" (52.1cm–55.9cm) circumference

Gauge

15 sts = 4" (10.2cm);
7 rows dc = 4" (10.2cm)

Glossary of Abbreviations

ch(s)	chain(s)
st(s)	stitch(es)
sl st	slip stitch
sp(s)	space(s)
beg	beginning
sk	skip
rep	repeat
rnd(s)	round(s)
sc	single crochet
hdc	half double crochet
dc	double crochet
*	repeat instructions following the asterisk as directed
( )	work instructions within the parentheses as many times as directed

Make the Scalloped Beanie *(0–3 months)*

Ch 4; join with sl st in 1st ch to form ring.

Rnd 1: Ch 3 (counts as dc now and throughout), work 11 dc in ring; join with sl st in 3rd ch of beg ch-3. (12 dc)

Rnd 2: Ch 3, dc in same st as joining, * 2 dc in next dc; rep from * around; join with sl st in 3rd ch of beg ch-3. (24 dc)

Rnd 3: Ch 3, 2 dc in next 2 dc, * dc in next dc, 2 dc in next 2 dc, rep from * around; join with sl st in 3rd ch of beg ch-3. (40 dc)

Rnd 4: Ch 1, sc in same st as joining, * ch 3, sk next 3 dc, sc in next dc, rep from * around to last 3 sts, ch 3, sk last 3 sts; join with sl st in beg sc. (10 ch sps)

Rnd 5: Ch 1, sc in same st as joining, 5 dc in next ch sp (scallop made), * sc in next sc, 5 dc in next ch sp, rep from * around; join with sl st in beg sc. (10 scallops)

Rnd 6: Ch 1, sk 1st dc, sl st in next dc, (sl st, ch 1, sc) in next dc, ch 3, sc in 3rd dc of next scallop, * ch 4, sc in 3rd dc of next scallop, ch 3, sc in 3rd dc of next scallop, rep from * around to last scallop, ch 4; join with sl st in beg sc. (10 ch sps)

Rnds 7–10: Rep Rnds 5 and 6.

For the regular beanie style, proceed with Rnds 11 and 12.

To add the optional Sunhat Brim: Fasten off, weave in ends and proceed with the Sunhat Brim instructions at the end of the chapter.

Rnd 11: Ch 1, sc in same st as joining, 3 sc in next ch sp, * sc in next sc, 3 sc in next ch sp, rep from * around; join with sl st in beg sc. (40 sc)

To add the optional Newsboy Brim: Fasten off, weave in ends and proceed with the Newsboy Brim instructions at the end of the chapter.

Rnd 12: Ch 1, sc in same st as joining and in each st around; join with sl st in beg sc. (40 sc)

Fasten off. Weave in ends.

For button placement, follow the instructions at the end of the project.

Make the Scalloped Beanie *(3–6 months)*

Ch 4; join with sl st in 1st ch to form ring.

Rnd 1: Ch 3 (counts as dc now and throughout), work 11 dc in ring; join with sl st in 3rd ch of beg ch-3 sp. (12 dc)

Rnd 2: Ch 3, dc in same st as joining, * 2 dc in next dc, rep from * around; join with sl st in 3rd ch of beg ch-3. (24 dc)

Rnd 3: Ch 3, 2 dc in next dc, * dc in next dc, 2 dc in next dc, rep from * around; join with sl st in 3rd ch of beg ch-3. (36 dc)

Rnd 4: Ch 3, dc in next 3 dc, 2 dc in next dc, * dc in next 4 dc, 2 dc in next dc, rep from * around to last st, dc in last st; join with sl st in 3rd ch of beg ch-3. (43 dc)

Rnd 5: Ch 1, sc in same st as joining, * ch 3, sk next 3 dc, sc in next dc, rep from * around to last 2 sts, ch 3, sk last 2 sts; join with sl st in beg sc. (11 ch sps)

Rnd 6: Ch 1, sc in same st as joining, 5 dc in next ch sp (scallop made), * sc in next sc, 5 dc in next ch sp, rep from * around; join with sl st in beg sc. (11 scallops)

Rnd 7: Ch 1, sk 1st dc, sl st in next dc, (sl st, ch 1, sc) in next dc, * ch 3, sc in 3rd dc of next scallop, ch 4, sc in 3rd dc of next scallop, rep from * around to last scallop, ch 3; join with sl st in beg sc. (11 ch sps)

Rnds 8–11: Rep Rnds 6 and 7.

For the regular beanie style, proceed with Rnds 12 and 13.

To add the optional Sunhat Brim: Fasten off, weave in ends and proceed with the Sunhat Brim instructions at the end of the chapter.

Rnd 12: Ch 1, sc in same st as joining, 3 sc in next ch sp, * sc in next sc, 3 sc in next ch sp, rep from * around; join with sl st in beg sc. (44 sc)

To add the optional Newsboy Brim: Fasten off, weave in ends and proceed with the Newsboy Brim instructions at the end of the chapter.

Rnd 13: Ch 1, sc in same st as joining and in each st around; join with sl st in beg sc. (44 sc)

Fasten off. Weave in ends.

For button placement, follow the instructions at the end of the project.

Make the Scalloped Beanie (6–12 months)

Ch 4; join with sl st in 1st ch to form ring.

Rnd 1: Ch 3 (counts as dc now and throughout), work 11 dc in ring; join with sl st in 3rd ch of beg ch-3. (12 dc)

Rnd 2: Ch 3, dc in same st as joining, * 2 dc in next dc, rep from * around; join with sl st in 3rd ch of beg ch-3. (24 dc)

Rnd 3: Ch 3, 2 dc in next dc, * dc in next dc, 2 dc in next dc, rep from * around; join with sl st in 3rd ch of beg ch-3. (36 dc)

Rnd 4: Ch 3, dc in next dc, 2 dc in next dc, * dc in next 2 dc, 2 dc in next dc, rep from * around; join with sl st in 3rd ch of beg ch-3. (48 dc)

Rnd 5: Ch 3, dc in next st and in each st around; join with sl st in 3rd ch of beg ch-3. (48 dc)

Rnd 6: Ch 2, hdc in next st and in each st around; join with sl st in 2nd ch of beg ch-2. (48 hdc)

Rnd 7: Ch 1, sc in same st as joining, * ch 3, sk next 3 hdc, sc in next hdc, rep from * around to last 3 sts, ch 3, sk last 3 sts; join with sl st in beg sc. (12 ch sps)

Rnd 8: Ch 1, sc in same st as joining, 5 dc in next ch sp (scallop made), * sc in next sc, 5 dc in next ch sp, rep from * around; join with sl st in beg sc. (12 scallops)

Rnd 9: Ch 1, sk 1st dc, sl st in next dc, (sl st, ch 1, sc) in next dc, ch 3, sc in 3rd dc of next scallop, * ch 4, sc in 3rd dc of next scallop, ch 3, sc in 3rd dc of next scallop, rep from * around to last scallop, ch 4; join with sl st in beg sc. (12 ch sps)

Rnds 10–13: Rep Rnds 8 and 9.

For the regular beanie style, proceed with Rnds 14 and 15.

To add the optional Sunhat Brim: Fasten off, weave in ends and proceed with the Sunhat Brim instructions at the end of the chapter.

Rnd 14: Ch 1, sc in same st as joining, 3 sc in next ch sp, * sc in next sc, 3 sc in next ch sp, rep from * around; join with sl st in beg sc. (48 sc)

To add the optional Newsboy Brim: Fasten off, weave in ends and proceed with the Newsboy Brim instructions at the end of the chapter.

Rnd 15: Ch 1, sc in same st as joining and in each st around; join with sl st in beg sc. (48 sc)

For button placement, follow the instructions at the end of the project.

Make the Scalloped Beanie *(1–3 years)*

Ch 4; join with sl st in 1st ch to form ring.

Rnd 1: Ch 3 (counts as dc now and throughout), work 11 dc in ring; join with sl st in 3rd ch of beg ch-3. (12 dc)

Rnd 2: Ch 3, dc in same st as joining, * 2 dc in next dc, rep from * around; join with sl st in 3rd ch of beg ch-3. (24 dc)

Rnd 3: Ch 3, 2 dc in next dc, * dc in next dc, 2 dc in next dc, rep from * around; join with sl st in 3rd ch of beg ch-3. (36 dc)

Rnd 4: Ch 3, dc in next dc, 2 dc in next dc, * dc in next 2 dc, 2 dc in next dc, rep from * around; join with sl st in 3rd ch of beg ch-3. (48 dc)

Rnd 5: Ch 2, hdc in next 7 dc, 2 hdc in next dc, * hdc in next 8 dc, 2 hdc in next dc, rep from * around to last 3 sts, hdc in last 3 sts; join with sl st in 2nd ch of beg ch-2. (53 hdc)

Rnd 6: Ch 1, sc in same st as joining, * ch 3, sk next 3 hdc, sc in next hdc, rep from * around to last 8 sts, (ch 3, sk next 2 sts, sc in next st) 2 times, ch 3, sk last 2 sts; join with sl st in beg sc. (14 ch sps)

Rnd 7: Ch 1, sc in same st as joining, 5 dc in next ch sp (scallop made), * sc in next sc, 5 dc in next ch sp, rep from * around; join with sl st in beg sc. (14 scallops)

Rnd 8: Ch 1, sk 1st dc, sl st in next dc, (sl st, ch 1, sc) in next dc, ch 3, sc in 3rd dc of next scallop, * ch 4, sc in 3rd dc of next scallop, ch 3, sc in 3rd dc of next scallop, rep from * around to last scallop, ch 4; join with sl st in beg sc. (14 ch sps)

Rnds 9–14: Rep Rnds 7 and 8.

For the regular beanie style, proceed with Rnds 15 and 16.

To add the optional Sunhat Brim: Fasten off, weave in ends and proceed with Sunhat Brim instructions at the end of the chapter.

Rnd 15: Ch 1, sc in same st as joining, 3 sc in next ch sp, * sc in next sc, 3 sc in next ch sp, rep from * around; join with sl st in beg sc. (56 sc)

To add the optional Newsboy Brim: Fasten off, weave in ends and proceed with the Newsboy Brim instructions at the end of the chapter.

Rnd 16: Ch 1, sc in same st as joining and in each st around; join with sl st in beg sc. (56 sc)

Fasten off. Weave in ends.

For button placement, follow the instructions at the end of the project.

Make the Scalloped Beanie *(4–8 years)*

Ch 4; join with sl st in 1st ch to form ring.

Rnd 1: Ch 3 (counts as dc now and throughout), work 11 dc in ring; join with sl st in 3rd ch of beg ch-3. (12 dc)

Rnd 2: Ch 3, dc in same st as joining, * 2 dc in next dc, rep from * around; join with sl st in 3rd ch of beg ch-3. (24 dc)

Rnd 3: Ch 3, 2 dc in next dc, * dc in next dc, 2 dc in next dc, rep from * around; join with sl st in 3rd ch of beg ch-3. (36 dc)

Rnd 4: Ch 3, dc in next dc, 2 dc in next dc, * dc in next 2 dc, 2 dc in next dc, rep from * around; join with sl st in 3rd ch of beg ch-3. (48 dc)

Rnd 5: Ch 3, dc in next 5 dc, 2 dc in next dc, * dc in next 6 dc, 2 dc in next dc, rep from * around to last 6 sts, dc in next 5 sts, 2 dc in last st; join with sl st in 3rd ch of beg ch-3. (55 dc)

Rnd 6: Ch 1, sc in same st as joining, * ch 3, sk next 3 dc, sc in next dc, rep from * around to last 10 sts, (ch 3, sk next 2 sts, sc in next st) 3 times, ch 3, sk last st; join with sl st in beg sc. (15 ch sps)

Rnd 7: Ch 1, sc in same st as joining, 5 dc in next ch sp (scallop made), * sc in next sc, 5 dc in next ch sp, rep from * around; join with sl st in beg sc. (15 scallops)

Rnd 8: Ch 1, sk 1st dc, sl st in next dc, (sl st, ch 1, sc) in next dc, * ch 3, sc in 3rd dc of next scallop, ch 4, sc in 3rd dc of next scallop, rep from * around to last scallop, ch 3; join with sl st in beg sc. (15 ch sps)

Rnds 9–14: Rep Rnds 7 and 8.

For the regular beanie style, proceed with Rnds 15 and 16.

To add the optional Sunhat Brim: Fasten off, weave in ends and proceed with the Sunhat Brim instructions at the end of the chapter.

Rnd 15: Ch 1, sc in same st as joining, 3 sc in next ch sp, * sc in next sc, 3 sc in next ch sp, rep from * around; join with sl st in beg sc. (60 sc)

To add the optional Newsboy Brim: Fasten off, weave in ends and proceed with the Newsboy Brim instructions at the end of the chapter.

Rnd 16: Ch 1, sc in same st as joining and in each st around; join with sl st in beg sc. (60 sc)

Fasten off. Weave in ends.

For button placement, follow the instructions at the end of the project.

Make the Scalloped Beanie (9 years–adult)

Ch 4; join with sl st in 1st ch to form ring.

Rnd 1: Ch 3 (counts as dc now and throughout), work 11 dc in ring; join with sl st in 3rd ch of beg ch-3. (12 dc)

Rnd 2: Ch 3, dc in same st as joining, * 2 dc in next dc, rep from * around; join with sl st in 3rd ch of beg ch-3. (24 dc)

Rnd 3: Ch 3, 2 dc in next dc, * dc in next dc, 2 dc in next dc, rep from * around; join with sl st in 3rd ch of beg ch-3. (36 dc)

Rnd 4: Ch 3, dc in next dc, 2 dc in next dc, * dc in next 2 dc, 2 dc in next dc, rep from * around; join with sl st in 3rd ch of beg ch-3. (48 dc)

Rnd 5: Ch 3, dc in next 3 dc, 2 dc in next dc, * dc in next 4 dc, 2 dc in next dc, rep from * around to last 3 sts, dc in next 2 sts, 2 dc in last st; join with sl st in 3rd ch of beg ch-3. (58 dc)

Rnd 6: Ch 2, hdc in next st and in each st around; join with sl st in 2nd ch of beg ch-2. (58 hdc)

Rnd 7: Ch 1, sc in same st as joining, * ch 3, sk next 3 hdc, sc next hdc, rep from * around to last 13 sts, (ch 3, sk next 2 sts, sc in next st) 4 times, ch 3, sk last st; join with sl st in beg sc. (16 ch sps)

Rnd 8: Ch 1, sc in same st as joining, 5 dc in next ch sp (scallop made), * sc in next sc, 5 dc in next ch sp, rep from * around; join with sl st in beg sc. (16 scallops)

Rnd 9: Ch 1, sk 1st dc, sl st in next dc, (sl st, ch 1, sc) in next dc, ch 3, sc in 3rd dc of next scallop, * ch 4, sc in 3rd dc of next scallop, ch 3, sc in 3rd dc of next scallop, rep from * around to last scallop, ch 4; join with sl st in beg sc. (16 ch sps)

Rnds 10–15: Rep Rnds 8 and 9.

For the regular beanie style, proceed with Rnds 16 and 17.

To add the optional Sunhat Brim: Fasten off, weave in ends and proceed with the Sunhat Brim instructions at the end of the chapter.

Rnd 16: Ch 1, sc in same st as joining, 3 sc in next ch sp, * sc in next sc, 3 sc in next ch sp, rep from * around; join with sl st in beg sc. (64 sc)

To add the optional Newsboy Brim: Fasten off, weave in ends and proceed with the Newsboy Brim instructions at the end of the chapter.

Rnd 17: Ch 1, sc in same st as joining and in each st round; join with sl st in beg sc. (64 sc)

For button placement, follow the instructions below.

Button Placement

Orient the joining seam of the hat toward the back. Sew the button 1"–1½" (2.5cm–3.8cm) from the bottom of the brim on one side.

For button placement on the variation brims, follow the instructions at the end of the chapter.

Droplet Beanie

Have an upcoming photo shoot for your little cherub? Why not make it more memorable by whipping up this delicate beanie to remember the occasion. The pictures will be priceless, and you will have memories to treasure forever. Modify the beanie by adding the Sunhat Brim or make one in coordinating colors to match your most adored sundress. This pattern works up quickly and ends in true beauty.

MATERIALS

For Droplet Beanie: Light sport weight yarn 〔 3 〕 in the color of your choice

- 0-3 mos. (80yd/73.2m)

- 3-6 mos. (90yd/82.3m)

- 6-12 mos. (110yd/100.6m)

- 1-3 yrs. (130yd/118.9m)

- 4-8 yrs. (140yd/128m)

- 9 yrs.-adult (160yd/146.3m)

For optional Sunhat Brim: Light sport weight yarn in the same color as the hat (100yd/91.4m)

Size I (5.5mm) crochet hook

⅞"-1" (2.2cm-2.5cm) button

Tapestry needle

Scissors

Finished Project Sizes

To fit approx. 0-3 months: 12"-13½" (30.5cm-34.3cm) circumference

To fit approx. 3-6 months: 14"-15" (35.6cm-38.1cm) circumference

To fit approx. 6-12 months: 15"-16½" (38.1cm-41.9cm) circumference

To fit approx. 1-3 years: 16½"-18" (41.9cm-45.7cm) circumference

To fit approx. 4-8 years: 18½"-20" (47cm-50.8cm) circumference

To fit approx. 9 years-adult: 20½"-22" (52.1cm-55.9cm) circumference

Gauge

15 sts = 4" (10.2cm);
7 rows dc = 4" (10.2cm)

Glossary of Abbreviations

ch(s)	chain(s)
st(s)	stitch(s)
sl st	slip stitch
sp(s)	space(s)
beg	beginning
rep	repeat
rnd(s)	round(s)
sc	single crochet
hdc	half double crochet
dc	double crochet
*	repeat instructions following the asterisk as directed
( )	work instructions within parentheses as many times as directed

Droplet Beanie (0–3 months)

Ch 4; join with sl st in 1st ch to form ring.

Rnd 1: Ch 3 (counts as dc now and throughout), work 11 dc in ring; join with sl st in 3rd ch of beg ch-3. (12 dc)

Rnd 2: Ch 3, dc in same st as joining, * 2 dc in next dc, rep from * around; join with sl st in 3rd ch of beg ch-3. (24 dc)

Rnd 3: Ch 3, 2 dc in next 2 dc, * dc in next dc, 2 dc in next 2 dc, rep from * around; join with sl st in 3rd ch of beg ch-3. (40 dc)

Rnd 4: Ch 1, sc in same st as joining, * ch 2, sk next 2 dc, sc in next dc, rep from * around to last 3 sts, ch 2, sk next st, sc in next st, ch 2, sk last st; join with sl st in beg sc. (14 ch-2 sps)

Rnd 5: Ch 1, sc in same st as joining, * (dc, ch 2, dc) in next ch-2 sp, sc in sc, rep from * around to last ch-2 sp, (dc, ch 2, dc) in last ch-2 sp; join with sl st in beg sc. (14 ch-2 sps)

Rnd 6: Ch 1, (sl st, ch 1, sc) in next ch-2 sp, ch 2, sc in next ch-2 sp, (ch 3, sc in next ch-2 sp, ch 2, sc in next ch-2 sp) 6 times, ch 3; join with sl st in beg sc. (14 ch-2 sps)

Rnds 7–12: Rep Rnds 5 and 6, ending on Rnd 5.

To continue with the scalloped edging round for the regular beanie style, proceed with Rnd 13.

To add the optional Sunhat Brim: Fasten off, weave in ends and proceed with the Sunhat Brim instructions at the end of the chapter.

Rnd 13: Ch 1, * (sl st, 2 dc, sl st) in next ch-2 sp (scallop made), rep from * around; join with sl st in beg ch-1. (14 scallops)

Fasten off. Weave in ends.

For button placement, follow the instructions at the end of the project.

Droplet Beanie *(3–6 months)*

Ch 4; join with sl st in 1st ch to form ring.

Rnd 1: Ch 3 (counts as dc now and throughout), work 11 dc in ring; join with sl st in 3rd ch of beg ch-3. (12 dc)

Rnd 2: Ch 3, dc in same st as joining, * 2 dc in next dc, rep from * around; join with sl st in 3rd ch of beg ch-3. (24 dc)

Rnd 3: Ch 3, 2 dc in next dc, * dc in next dc, 2 dc in next dc, rep from * around; join with sl st in 3rd ch of beg ch-3. (36 dc)

Rnd 4: Ch 3, dc in next 3 dc, 2 dc in next dc, * dc in next 4 dc, 2 dc in next dc, rep from * around to last st, dc in last st; join with sl st in 3rd ch of beg ch-3. (43 dc)

Rnd 5: Ch 1, sc in same st as joining, * ch 2, sk next 2 dc, sc in next dc, rep from * around to last 3 sts, ch 2, sk next st, sc in next st, ch 2, sk last st; join with sl st in beg sc. (15 ch-2 sps)

Rnd 6: Ch 1, sc in same st as joining, * (dc, ch 2, dc) in next ch sp, sc in sc, rep from * around to last ch sp, (dc, ch 2, dc) in last ch sp; join with sl st in beg sc. (15 ch-2 sps)

Rnd 7: Ch 1, (sl st, ch 1, sc) in next ch-2 sp, (ch 2, sc in next ch-2 sp, ch 3, sc in next ch-2 sp) 7 times, ch 2; join with sl st in beg sc. (15 ch-2 sps)

Rnds 8–13: Rep Rnds 6 and 7.

To continue with the scalloped edging round for the regular beanie style, proceed with Rnd 14.

To add the optional Sunhat Brim: Fasten off, weave in ends and proceed with the Sunhat Brim instructions at the end of the chapter.

Rnd 14: Ch 1, * (sl st, 2 dc, sl st) in next ch-2 sp (scallop made), rep from * around; join with sl st in beg ch-1. (15 scallops)

Fasten off. Weave in ends.

For button placement, follow the instructions at the end of the project.

Droplet Beanie *(6–12 months)*

Ch 4; join with sl st in 1st ch to form ring.

Rnd 1: Ch 3 (counts as dc now and throughout), work 11 dc in ring; join with sl st in 3rd ch of beg ch-3. (12 dc)

Rnd 2: Ch 3, dc in same st as joining, * 2 dc in next dc, rep from * around; join with sl st in 3rd ch of beg ch-3. (24 dc)

Rnd 3: Ch 3, 2 dc in next dc, * dc in next dc, 2 dc in next dc, rep from * around; join with sl st in 3rd ch of beg ch-3. (36 dc)

Rnd 4: Ch 3, dc in next dc, 2 dc in next dc, * dc in next 2 dc, 2 dc in next dc, rep from * around; join with sl st in 3rd ch of beg ch-3. (48 dc)

Rnd 5: Ch 2, hdc in next st and in each st around; join with sl st in 2nd ch of beg ch-2. (48 hdc)

Rnd 6: Ch 1, sc in same st as joining, * ch 2, sk next 2 hdc, sc in next hdc, rep from * around to last 2 sts, ch 2, sk last 2 sts; join with sl st in beg sc. (16 ch-2 sps)

Rnd 7: Ch 1, sc in same st as joining, * (dc, ch 2, dc) in next ch-2 sp, sc in sc, rep from * around to last ch-2 sp, (dc, ch 2, dc) in last ch-2 sp; join with sl st in beg sc. (16 ch-2 sps)

Rnd 8: Ch 1, (sl st, ch 1, sc) in next ch-2 sp, ch 2, sc in next ch-2 sp, (ch 3, sc in next ch-2 sp, ch 2, sc in next ch-2 sp) 7 times, ch 3; join with sl st in beg sc. (16 ch-2 sps)

Rnds 9–14: Rep Rnds 7 and 8.

To continue with the scalloped edging round for the regular beanie style, proceed with Rnd 15.

To add the optional Sunhat Brim: Fasten off, weave in ends and proceed with the Sunhat Brim instructions at the end of the chapter.

Rnd 15: Ch 1, * (sl st, 2 dc, sl st) in next ch sp (scallop made), rep from * around; join with sl st in beg ch-1. (16 scallops)

Fasten off. Weave in ends.

For button placement, follow the instructions at the end of the project.

Droplet Beanie *(1–3 years)*

Ch 4; join with sl st in 1st ch to form ring.

Rnd 1: Ch 3 (counts as dc now and throughout), work 11 dc in ring; join with sl st in 3rd ch of beg ch-3. (12 dc)

Rnd 2: Ch 3, dc in same st as joining, * 2 dc in next dc, rep from * around; join with sl st in 3rd ch of beg ch-3. (24 dc)

Rnd 3: Ch 3, 2 dc in next dc, * dc in next dc, 2 dc in next dc, rep from * around; join with sl st in 3rd ch of beg ch-3. (36 dc)

Rnd 4: Ch 3, dc in next dc, 2 dc in next dc, * dc in next 2 dc, 2 dc in next dc, rep from * around; join with sl st in 3rd ch of beg ch-3. (48 dc)

Rnd 5: Ch 2, hdc in next 7 dc, 2 hdc in next dc, * hdc in next 8 dc, 2 hdc in next dc, rep from * around to last 3 sts, hdc in last 3 sts; join with sl st in 2nd ch of beg ch-2. (53 hdc)

Rnd 6: Ch 1, sc in same st as joining, * ch 2, sk next 2 hdc, sc in next hdc, rep from * around to last st, ch 2, sk last st; join with sl st in beg sc. (18 ch-2 sps)

Rnd 7: Ch 1, sc in same st as joining, * (dc, ch 2, dc) in next ch-2 sp, sc in sc, rep from * around to last ch-2 sp, (dc, ch 2, dc) in last ch-2 sp; join with sl st in beg sc. (18 ch-2 sps)

Rnd 8: Ch 1, (sl st, ch 1, sc) in next ch-2 sp, ch 2, sc in next ch-2 sp, (ch 3, sc in next ch-3 sp, ch 2, sc in next ch-2 sp) 8 times, ch 3, join with sl st in beg sc. (18 ch-2 sps)

Rnds 9–16: Rep Rnds 7 and 8.

To continue with the scalloped edging round for the regular beanie style, proceed with Rnd 17.

To add the optional Sunhat Brim: Fasten off, weave in ends and proceed with the Sunhat Brim instructions at the end of the chapter.

Rnd 17: Ch 1, * (sl st, 2 dc, sl st) in next ch-2 sp (scallop made), rep from * around; join with sl st in beg ch-1. (18 scallops)

Fasten off. Weave in ends.

For button placement, follow the instructions at the end of the project.

Droplet Beanie *(4–8 years)*

Ch 4; join with sl st in 1st ch to form ring.

Rnd 1: Ch 3 (counts as dc now and throughout), work 11 dc in ring; join with sl st in 3rd ch of beg ch-3. (12 dc)

Rnd 2: Ch 3, dc in same st as joining, * 2 dc in next dc, rep from * around; join with sl st in 3rd ch of beg ch-3. (24 dc)

Rnd 3: Ch 3, 2 dc in next dc, * dc in next dc, 2 dc in next dc, rep from * around; join with sl st in 3rd ch of beg ch-3. (36 dc)

Rnd 4: Ch 3, dc in next dc, 2 dc in next dc, * dc in next 2 dc, 2 dc in next dc, rep from * around; join with sl st in 3rd ch of beg ch-3. (48 dc)

Rnd 5: Ch 3, dc in next 5 dc, 2 dc in next dc, * dc in next 6 dc, 2 dc in next dc, rep from * around to last 6 sts, dc in next 5 sts, 2 dc in last st; join with sl st in 3rd ch of beg ch-3. (55 dc)

Rnd 6: Ch 2, hdc in next st and in each st around; join with sl st in 2nd ch of beg ch-2. (55 hdc)

Rnd 7: Ch 1, sc in same st as joining, * ch 2, sk next 2 hdc, sc in next hdc, rep from * around to last 3 sts, ch 2, sk next st, sc in next st, ch 2, sk last st; join with sl st in beg sc. (19 ch-2 sps)

Rnd 8: Ch 1, sc in same st as joining, * (dc, ch 2, dc) in next ch-2 sp, sc in sc, rep from * around to last ch-2 sp, (dc, ch 2, dc) in last ch-2 sp; join with sl st in beg sc. (19 ch-2 sps)

Rnd 9: Ch 1, (sl st, ch 1, sc) in next ch-2 sp, (ch 2, sc in next ch sp, ch 3, sc in next ch sp) 9 times, ch 2; join with sl st in beg sc. (19 ch sps)

Rnds 10–17: Rep Rnds 8 and 9.

To continue with the scalloped edging round for the regular beanie style, proceed with Rnd 18.

To add the optional Sunhat Brim: Fasten off, weave in ends and proceed with the Sunhat Brim instructions at the end of the chapter.

Rnd 18: Ch 1, * (sl st, 2 dc, sl st) in next ch sp (scallop made), rep from * around; join with sl st in beg ch-1. (19 scallops)

Fasten off. Weave in ends.

For button placement, follow the instructions at the end of the project.

Droplet Beanie *(9 years–adult)*

Ch 4; join with sl st in 1st ch to form ring.

Rnd 1: Ch 3 (counts as dc now and throughout), work 11 dc in ring; join with sl st in 3rd ch of beg ch-3. (12 dc)

Rnd 2: Ch 3, dc in same st as joining, * 2 dc in next dc, rep from * around, join with sl st in 3rd ch of beg ch-3. (24 dc)

Rnd 3: Ch 3, 2 dc in next dc, * dc in next dc, 2 dc in next dc, rep from * around; join with sl st in 3rd ch of beg ch-3. (36 dc)

Rnd 4: Ch 3, dc in next dc, 2 dc in next dc, * dc in next 2 dc, 2 dc in next dc, rep from * around; join with sl st in 3rd ch of beg ch-3. (48 dc)

Rnd 5: Ch 3, dc in next 3 dc, 2 dc in next dc, * dc in next 4 dc, 2 dc in next dc, rep from * around to last 3 sts, dc in next 2 sts, 2 dc in last st; join with sl st in 3rd ch of beg ch-3. (58 dc)

Rnd 6: Ch 3, dc in next st and in each st around; join with sl st in 3rd ch of beg ch-3. (58 dc)

Rnd 7: Ch 1, sc in same st as joining, * ch 2, sk next 2 dc, sc in next dc, rep from * around to last 3 sts, ch 2, sk next st, sc in next st, ch 2, sk last st; join with sl st in beg sc. (20 ch-2 sps)

Rnd 8: Ch 1, sc in same st as joining, * (dc, ch 2, dc) in next ch-2 sp, sc in sc, rep from * around to last ch-2 sp, (dc, ch 2, dc) in last ch-2 sp; join with sl st in beg sc. (20 ch-2 sps)

Rnd 9: Ch 1 (sl st, ch 1, sc) in next ch-2 sp, ch 2, sc in next ch-2 sp, (ch 3, sc in next ch-2 sp, ch 2, sc in next ch-2 sp) 9 times, ch 3, join with sl st in beg sc. (20 ch-2 sps)

Rnds 10–17: Rep Rnds 8 and 9.

To continue with the scalloped edging round for the regular beanie style, proceed with Rnd 18.

To add the optional Sunhat Brim: Fasten off, weave in ends and proceed with the Sunhat Brim instructions at the end of the chapter.

Rnd 18: Ch 1, * (sl st, 2 dc, sl st) in next ch-2 sp (scallop made), rep from * around; join with sl st in beg ch-1. (20 scallops)

Fasten off. Weave in ends.

For button placement, follow the instructions below.

Button Placement

Orient the joining seam of the hat toward the back. Sew the button 1"–1½" (2.5cm–3.8cm) from the bottom of the brim on one side.

For button placement on the Sunhat Brim, follow the instructions at the end of the chapter.

Twisted Beanie

The puff stitches in this hat make it truly unique, and although this pattern is for the more experienced crocheter, with the illustrations and some patience, you will be working it up in no time. Wear this hat all year long—while dressed up, in your favorite pair of jeans or to your first day of school. Add a Newsboy Brim for a subtle look, Earflaps for the cooler fall and winter days or wear it as a simple, stylish beanie. Picture your little troopers playing in their treehouse, wearing a snuggly hat with earflaps. Match it to their favorite jacket or scarf, and you won't have to persuade them to bundle up again.

MATERIALS

For Twisted Beanie: Light sport weight yarn (3) in the color of your choice

- 0–3 mos. (100yd/91.4m)
- 3–6 mos. (110yd/100.6m)
- 6–12 mos. (130yd/118.9m)
- 1–3 yrs. (150yd/137.2m)
- 4–8 yrs. (160yd/146.3m)
- 9 yrs.–adult (180yd/164.6m)

For optional Newsboy Brim: Light sport weight yarn in the same color as the hat (18yd/16.5m)

For optional Earflaps: Light sport weight yarn in the same color as the hat (44yd/40.2m)

Size I (5.5mm) crochet hook

⅞"–1" (2.2cm–2.5cm) button

Tapestry needle

Scissors

Finished Project Sizes

To fit approx. 0–3 months: 12"–13½" (30.5cm–34.3cm) circumference

To fit approx. 3–6 months: 14"–15" (35.6cm–38.1cm) circumference

To fit approx. 6–12 months: 15"–16½" (38.1cm–41.9cm) circumference

To fit approx. 1–3 years: 16½"–18" (41.9cm–45.7cm) circumference

To fit approx. 4–8 years: 18½"–20" (47cm–50.8cm) circumference

To fit approx. 9 years–adult: 20½"–22" (52.1cm–55.9cm) circumference

Gauge

15 sts = 4" (10.2cm);
7 rows dc = 4" (10.2cm)

Glossary of Abbreviations

ch(s)	chain(s)
st(s)	stitch(s)
sl st	slip stitch
sp(s)	space(s)
beg	beginning
sk	skip
rep	repeat
yoh	yarn over hook
rnd(s)	round(s)
bpdc	back post double crochet
sc	single crochet
hdc	half double crochet
dc	double crochet
PS	puff stitch
*	repeat instructions following the asterisk as directed
( )	work instructions within parentheses as many times as directed

Twisted Beanie *(0–3 months)*

Ch 4; join with sl st in 1st ch to form ring.

Rnd 1: Ch 3, dc in same st as joining, * 2 dc in next dc, rep from * around; join with sl st in 3rd ch of beg ch-3. (24 dc)

Rnd 2: Ch 3, dc in same dc as joining, * 2 dc in next dc, rep from * around; join with sl st in 3rd ch of beg ch-3. (24 dc)

Rnd 3: Ch 3, 2 dc in next 2 dc, * dc in next dc, 2 dc in next 2 dc, rep from * around; join with sl st in 3rd ch of beg ch-3. (40 dc)

Rnd 4: Ch 2, hdc in next st and in each st around; join with sl st in 2nd ch of beg ch-2. (40 hdc)

Rnd 5 (Puff Stitch Rnd): Ch 5, PS in next st, sk next 2 sts, * (dc, ch 2, PS) in next st, sk next 2 sts, rep from * around; join with sl st in 3rd ch of beg ch-5. (13 PS)

Rnd 6: Ch 1, 3 sc in next ch-2 sp, work 1 bpdc around the post of the next unworked st in the round before the Puff Stitch Rnd, * 2 sc in next ch-2 sp. Work 1 bpdc around the post of the next unworked st in the round before the Puff Stitch Rnd, rep from * around; join with sl st in beg sc. (40 sts)

Rnd 7: Ch 3, dc in next st and in each st around; join with sl st in 3rd ch of beg ch-3. (40 dc)

Rnds 8–12: Rep Rnds 5–7, ending on Rnd 6.

Rnd 13: Ch 2, hdc in next st and in each st around; join with sl st in 2nd ch of beg ch-2. (40 hdc)

Snug Rnd (this round prevents the brim of the hat from stretching): Ch 1, sc in same st as joining, sl st in next 2 hdc, * sc in next hdc, sl st in next 2 hdc, rep from * around to last st, sc in last st; join with sl st in beg sc. (40 sts)

Fasten off. Weave in ends.

For button placement and the optional Earflaps, follow the instructions at the end of the project.

To add the optional Newsboy Brim, see the instructions at the end of the chapter.

To learn the Puff Stitch (PS), see Stitches & Techniques on page 14.

Twisted Beanie *(3–6 months)*

Ch 4; join with sl st in 1st ch to form ring.

Rnd 1: Ch 3 (counts as dc now and throughout), work 11 dc in ring; join with sl st in 3rd ch of beg ch-3 sp. (12 dc)

Rnd 2: Ch 3, dc in same st as joining, * 2 dc in next dc, rep from * around; join with sl st in 3rd ch of beg ch-3. (24 dc)

Rnd 3: Ch 3, 2 dc in next dc, * dc in next dc, 2 dc in next dc, rep from * around; join with sl st in 3rd ch of beg ch-3. (36 dc)

Rnd 4: Ch 3, dc in next 3 dc, 2 dc in next dc, * dc in next 4 dc, 2 dc in next dc, rep from * around to last st, dc in last st; join with sl st in 3rd ch of beg ch-3. (43 dc)

Rnd 5: Ch 2, hdc in next st and in each st around; join with sl st in 2nd ch of beg ch-2. (43 hdc)

Rnd 6 (Puff Stitch Rnd): Ch 5, PS in next st, sk next 2 sts, * (dc, ch 2, PS) in next st, sk next 2 sts, rep from * around; join with sl st in 3rd ch of beg ch-5. (14 PS)

Rnd 7: Ch 1, 3 sc in next ch-2 sp, work 1 bpdc around the post of the next unworked st in the round before the Puff Stitch Rnd, * 2 sc in next ch-2 sp. Work 1 bpdc around the post of the next unworked st in the round before the Puff Stitch Rnd, rep from * around; join with sl st in beg sc. (43 sts)

Rnd 8: Ch 3, dc in next st and in each st around; join with sl st in 3rd ch of beg ch-3. (43 dc)

Rnds 9–13: Rep Rnds 6–8, ending on Rnd 7.

Rnd 14: Ch 2, hdc in next st and in each st around; join with sl st in 2nd ch of beg ch-2. (43 hdc)

Snug Rnd (this round prevents the brim of the hat from stretching): Ch 1, sc in same st as joining, sl st in next 2 hdc, * sc in next hdc, sl st in next 2 hdc, rep from * around to last st, sc in last st; join with sl st in beg sc. (43 sts)

Fasten off. Weave in ends.

For button placement and the optional Earflaps, follow the instructions at the end of the project.

To add the optional Newsboy Brim, see the instructions at the end of the chapter.

Twisted Beanie *(6–12 months)*

Ch 4; join with sl st in 1st ch to form ring.

Rnd 1: Ch 3 (counts as dc now and throughout), work 11 dc in ring; join with sl st in 3rd ch of beg ch-3. (12 dc)

Rnd 2: Ch 3, dc in same st as joining, * 2 dc in next dc, rep from * around; join with sl st in 3rd ch of beg ch-3. (24 dc)

Rnd 3: Ch 3, 2 dc in next dc, * dc in next dc, 2 dc in next dc, rep from * around; join with sl st in 3rd ch of beg ch-3. (36 dc)

Rnd 4: Ch 3, dc in next dc, 2 dc in next dc, * dc in next 2 dc, 2 dc in next dc, rep from * around; join with sl st in 3rd ch of beg ch-3. (48 dc)

Rnds 5–6: Ch 3, dc in next st and in each st around; join with sl st in 3rd ch of beg ch-3. (48 dc)

Rnd 7 (Puff Stitch Rnd): Ch 5, PS in next st, * sk next 2 sts, (dc, ch 2, PS) in next st, rep from * around to last st, sk last st, join with sl st in 3rd ch of beg ch-5. (16 PS)

Rnd 8: Ch 1, 2 sc in next ch-2 sp, work 1 bpdc around the post of the next unworked st in the round before the Puff Stitch Rnd, * 2 sc in next ch-2 sp. Work 1 bpdc around the post of the next unworked st in the round before the Puff Stitch Rnd, rep from * around; join with sl st in beg sc. (48 sts)

Rnd 9: Ch 3, dc in next st and in each st around; join with sl st in 3rd ch of beg ch-3. (48 dc)

Rnds 10–14: Rep Rnds 7–9, ending on Rnd 8.

Rnd 15: Ch 2, hdc in next st and in each st around; join with sl st in 2nd ch of beg ch-2. (48 hdc)

Snug Rnd (this round prevents the brim of the hat from stretching): Ch 1, sc in same st as joining, sl st in next 2 hdc, * sc in next hdc, sl st in next 2 hdc, rep from * around; join with sl st in beg sc. (48 sts)

Fasten off. Weave in ends.

For button placement and the optional earflaps, follow the instructions at the end of the project.

To add the optional Newsboy Brim, see the instructions at the end of the chapter.

Twisted Beanie *(1–3 years)*

Ch 4; join with sl st in 1st ch to form ring.

Rnd 1: Ch 3 (counts as dc now and throughout), work 11 dc in ring; join with sl st in 3rd ch of beg ch-3. (12 dc)

Rnd 2: Ch 3, dc in same st as joining, * 2 dc in next dc; rep from * around; join with sl st in 3rd ch of beg ch-3. (24 dc)

Rnd 3: Ch 3, 2 dc in next dc, * dc in next dc, 2 dc in next dc, rep from * around; join with sl st in 3rd ch of beg ch-3. (36 dc)

Rnd 4: Ch 3, dc in next dc, 2 dc in next dc, * dc in next 2 dc, 2 dc in next dc, rep from * around; join with sl st in 3rd ch of beg ch-3. (48 dc)

Rnd 5: Ch 2, hdc in next 14 dc, 2 hdc in next dc, * hdc in next 15 dc, 2 hdc in next dc, rep from * around; join with sl st in 2nd ch of beg ch-2. (51 hdc)

Rnd 6 (Puff Stitch Rnd): Ch 5, PS in next st, * sk next 2 sts, (dc, ch 2, PS) in next st, rep from * around to last st, sk last st, join with sl st in 3rd ch of beg ch-5. (17 PS)

Rnd 7: Ch 1, 2 sc in next ch-2 sp, work 1 bpdc around the post of the next unworked st in the round before the Puff Stitch Rnd, * 2 sc in next ch-2 sp. Work 1 bpdc around the post of the next unworked st in the round before the Puff Stitch Rnd, rep from * around; join with sl st in beg sc. (51 sts)

Rnd 8: Ch 3, dc in next st and in each st around; join with sl st in 3rd ch of beg ch-3. (51 dc)

Rnds 9–16: Rep Rnds 6–8, ending on Rnd 7.

Rnd 17: Ch 2, hdc in next st and in each st around; join with sl st in 2nd ch of beg ch-2. (51 hdc)

Snug Rnd (this round prevents the brim of hat from stretching): Ch 1, sc in same st as joining, sl st in next 2 hdc, * sc in next hdc, sl st in next 2 hdc, rep from * around; join with sl st in beg sc. (51 sts)

Fasten off. Weave in ends.

For button placement and the optional Earflaps, follow the instructions at the end of the project.

To add the optional Newsboy Brim, see the instructions at the end of the chapter.

Twisted Beanie *(4–8 years)*

Ch 4; join with sl st in 1st ch to form ring.

Rnd 1: Ch 3 (counts as dc now and throughout), work 11 dc in ring; join with sl st in 3rd ch of beg ch-3. (12 dc)

Rnd 2: Ch 3, dc in same st as joining, * 2 dc in next dc, rep from * around; join with sl st in 3rd ch of beg ch-3. (24 dc)

Rnd 3: Ch 3, 2 dc in next dc, * dc in next dc, 2 dc in next dc, rep from * around; join with sl st in 3rd ch of beg ch-3. (36 dc)

Rnd 4: Ch 3, dc in next dc, 2 dc in next dc, * dc in next 2 dc, 2 dc in next dc, rep from * around; join with sl st in 3rd ch of beg ch-3. (48 dc)

Rnd 5: Ch 3, dc in next 5 dc, 2 dc in next dc, * dc in next 6 dc, 2 dc in next dc, rep from * around to last 6 sts, dc in next 5 sts, 2 dc in last st; join with sl st in 3rd ch of beg ch-3. (55 dc)

Rnd 6: Ch 3, dc in next st and in each st around; join with sl st in 3rd ch of beg ch-3. (55 dc)

Rnd 7 (Puff Stitch Rnd): Ch 5, PS in next st, sk next 2 sts, * (dc, ch 2, PS) in next st, sk next 2 sts, rep from * around; join with sl st in 3rd ch of beg ch-5. (18 PS)

Rnd 8: Ch 1, 3 sc in next ch-2 sp, work 1 bpdc around the post of the next unworked st in the round before the Puff Stitch Rnd, * 2 sc in next ch-2 sp. Work 1 bpdc around the post of the next unworked st in the round before the Puff Stitch Rnd, rep from * around; join with sl st in beg sc. (55 sts)

Rnd 9: Ch 3, dc in next st and in each st around; join with sl st in 3rd ch of beg ch-3. (55 dc)

Rnds 10–17: Rep Rnds 7–9, ending on Rnd 8.

Rnd 18: Ch 2, hdc in next st and in each st around; join with sl st in 2nd ch of beg ch-2. (55 hdc)

Snug Rnd (this round prevents the brim of the hat from stretching): Ch 1, sc in same st as joining, sl st in next 2 hdc, * sc in next hdc, sl st in next 2 hdc, rep from * around to last st, sc in last st; join with sl st in beg sc. (55 sts)

Fasten off. Weave in ends.

For button placement and the optional Earflaps, follow the instructions at the end of the project.

To add the optional Newsboy Brim, see the instructions at the end of the chapter.

Twisted Beanie *(9 years–adult)*

Ch 4; join with sl st in 1st ch to form ring.

Rnd 1: Ch 3 (counts as dc now and throughout), work 11 dc in ring; join with sl st in 3rd ch of beg ch-3. (12 dc)

Rnd 2: Ch 3, dc in same st as joining, * 2 dc in next dc, rep from * around; join with sl st in 3rd ch of beg ch-3. (24 dc)

Rnd 3: Ch 3, 2 dc in next dc, * dc in next dc, 2 dc in next dc, rep from * around; join with sl st in 3rd ch of beg ch-3. (36 dc)

Rnd 4: Ch 3, dc in next dc, 2 dc in next dc, * dc in next 2 dc, 2 dc in next dc, rep from * around; join with sl st in 3rd ch of beg ch-3. (48 dc)

Rnd 5: Ch 3, dc in next 3 dc, 2 dc in next dc, * dc in next 4 dc, 2 dc in next dc, rep from * around to last 3 sts, dc in next 2 sts, 2 dc in last st; join with sl st in 3rd ch of beg ch-3. (58 dc)

Rnd 6: Ch 3, dc in next st and in each st around; join with sl st in 3rd ch of beg ch-3. (58 dc)

Rnd 7 (Puff Stitch Rnd): Ch 5, PS in next st, sk next 2 sts, * (dc, ch 2, PS) in next st, sk next 2 sts, rep from * around; join with sl st in 3rd ch of beg ch-5. (19 PS)

Rnd 8: Ch 1, 3 sc in next ch-2 sp, work 1 bpdc around the post of the next unworked st in the round before the Puff Stitch Rnd, * 2 sc in next ch-2 sp. Work 1 bpdc around the post of the next unworked st in the round before the Puff Stitch

Rnd, rep from * around; join with sl st in beg sc. (58 sts)

Rnd 9: Ch 3, dc in next st and in each st around, join with sl st in 3rd ch of beg ch-3. (58 dc)

Rnds 10-17: Rep Rnds 7–9, ending on Rnd 8.

Rnd 18: Ch 2, hdc in next st and in each st around; join with sl st in 2nd ch of beg ch-2. (58 hdc)

Snug Rnd (this round prevents the brim of the hat from stretching): Ch 1, sc in same st as joining, sl st in next 2 hdc, * sc in next hdc, sl st in next 2 hdc, rep from * around to last st, sc in last st; join with sl st in beg sc. (58 sts)

Fasten off. Weave in ends.

For button placement and the optional Earflaps, follow the instructions below and on the following pages.

To add the optional Newsboy Brim, see the instructions at the end of the chapter.

Button Placement

Orient the joining seam of the hat toward the back. Sew the button 1"–1½" (2.5cm–3.8cm) from the bottom of the brim on one side. Attach the motif of your choice from Chapter 2 to the button.

For button placement on the variation brims, follow the instructions at the end of the chapter.

Add Earflaps to Your Twisted Beanie

Earflap Placement

Cut 2 small pieces of yarn to use as stitch markers.

With the front side of the hat facing up and the joining seam centered at the bottom, slip one piece of scrap yarn (first stitch marker) through the hdc st on the brim's left corner (in the Row before the Snug Rnd), then slip the other piece of scrap yarn (second stitch marker) through the hdc st on the brim's right corner (in the Row before the Snug Rnd).

Joining Slip Stitches for the Earflaps: You will be working all of the ending joining sts and sl sts in the last hdc round of the brim (round before the Snug Rnd).

Earflaps for sizes 0–3 months / 3–6 months / 6–12 months

Position the hat and the stitch markers as directed under Earflap Placement.

With the top of hat facing you, place the hook in 2nd hdc st to the right of either stitch marker; join new yarn.

Row 1: Yoh, work 9 dc in st marker st; join with sl st in 2nd hdc, then sl st in next 2 hdc. (9 dc)

Row 2: Turn, yoh, dc in next dc, (2 dc in next dc, dc in next dc) 4 times; join with sl st in 2nd hdc, sl st in next hdc. (13 dc)

Row 3: Turn, (2 sc in next dc, sc in next dc) 3 times, sc in next dc, ch 50, hdc in 2nd ch from hook and in each ch to the end, sc in same st where ch began, (sc in next dc, 2 sc in next dc) 3 times; join with sl st in the next hdc st. (20 sc).

Fasten off. Weave in ends.

Repeat hook placement and Rows 1–3 for the other earflap.

Earflaps for sizes: 1–3 years / 4–8 years / 9 years–adult

Position the hat and the stitch markers as directed under Earflap Placement.

With the top of the hat facing you, place hook in 2nd hdc st to the right of the stitch marker; join new yarn.

Row 1: Yoh, work 9 dc in st marker st; join with sl st in 2nd hdc, then sl st in next 2 hdc. (9 dc)

Row 2: Turn, yoh, dc in next dc, (2 dc in next dc, dc in next dc) 4 times; join with sl st in 2nd hdc, sl st in next hdc. (13 dc)

Row 3: Turn, (2 hdc in next dc, hdc in next dc) 3 times, hdc in next dc, ch 50, hdc in 2nd ch from hook and in each ch to the end, hdc in same st where ch began, (hdc in next dc, 2 hdc in next dc) 3 times; join with sl st in the next hdc st. (20 hdc)

Fasten off. Weave in ends.

Repeat hook placement and Rows 1–3 for the other earflap.

Trendy Slouch Hat

Let your inner diva shine through with this modern take on a classic. Wear it with your hair in or out, with a glitzy flower or simply on its own. Slouch hats are trendy and fashionable, and I've designed this one with comfort in mind by creating an adjustable brim for the perfect fit.

MATERIALS

For Trendy Slouch Hat: Light sport weight yarn 🧶 in the color of your choice

- 0–3 mos. (138yd/126.2m)
- 3–6 mos. (148yd/135.3m)
- 6–12 mos. (158yd/144.5m)
- 1–3 yrs. (168yd/153.6m)
- 4–8 yrs. (178yd/162.8m)
- 9 yrs.–adult (188yd/171.9m)

Size I (5.5mm) crochet hook

⅞"–1" (2.2cm–2.5cm) button

Tapestry needle

Scissors

Finished Project Sizes

To fit approx. 0–3 months: 12"–13½" (30.5cm–34.3cm) circumference

To fit approx. 3–6 months: 14"–15" (35.6cm–38.1cm) circumference

To fit approx. 6–12 months: 15"–16½" (38.1cm–41.9cm) circumference

To fit approx. 1–3 years: 16½"–18" (41.9cm–45.7cm) circumference

To fit approx. 4–8 years: 18½"–20" (47cm–50.8cm) circumference

To fit approx. 9 years–adult: 20½"–22" (52.1cm–55.9cm) circumference

Gauge

15 sts = 4" (10.2cm);
7 rows dc = 4" (10.2cm)

Glossary of Abbreviations

ch(s)	chain(s)
st(s)	stitch(s)
sl st	slip stitch
sp(s)	space(s)
beg	beginning
rem	remaining
rep	repeat
rnd(s)	round(s)
yoh	yarn over hook
sc	single crochet
hdc	half double crochet
dc	double crochet
tc	treble crochet
3dc-cl	3 double crochet cluster
V-st	treble crochet v-stitch
*	repeat instructions following the asterisk as directed
( )	work instructions within the parentheses as many times as directed

Trendy Slouch Hat (0–3 months)

Ch 4; join with sl st in 1st ch to form ring.

Rnd 1: Ch 3 (counts as dc now and throughout), work 11 dc in ring; join with sl st in 3rd ch of beg ch-3. (12 dc)

Rnd 2: Ch 3, dc in same st as joining, * 2 dc in next dc, rep from * around; join with sl st in 3rd ch of beg ch-3. (24 dc)

Rnd 3: Ch 3, 2 dc in next 2 dc, * dc in next dc, 2 dc in next 2 dc, rep from * around; join with sl st in 3rd ch of beg ch-3. (40 dc)

Rnd 4: Ch 1, sc in same st as joining, * ch 2, sk next 2 dc, sc in next dc, rep from * around to last 3 sts, ch 2, sk next st, sc in next st, ch 2, sk last st; join with sl st in beg sc. (14 ch-2 sps)

Rnd 5: Ch 1, working in 1st ch-2 sp, sl st, ch 2, (yoh, insert hook in same ch-2 sp, draw up loop, yoh, pull yarn through 2 loops on hook) 2 times, yoh, draw through rem 3 loops on hook, ch 3, 3dc-cl in same ch-2 sp, ch 1, * (3dc-cl, ch 3, 3dc-cl, ch 1) in next ch-2 sp, rep from * around; join with sl st in beg 3dc-cl. (28 3dc-cl)

Rnd 6: Ch 1, (sl st, ch 7, tc) in 1st ch-3 sp, * (tc, ch 3, tc) (V-st made) in next ch-3 sp, rep from * around; join with sl st in 4th ch of beg ch-7. (14 V-sts)

Rnd 7: Ch 1, working in 1st ch-3 sp, sl st, ch 2, (yoh, insert hook in same ch-3 sp, draw up loop, yoh, pull yarn through 2 loops on hook) 2 times, yoh, draw through rem 3 loops on hook, ch 3, 3dc-cl in same ch-3 sp, ch 1, * (3dc-cl, ch 3, 3dc-cl, ch 1) in next ch-3 sp, rep from * around; join with sl st in beg 3dc-cl. (28 3dc-cl)

Rnd 8: Rep Rnd 6.

Rnd 9: Ch 1, sc in same st as joining, 2 sc in 1st ch-3 sp, * sc in ch st between 2 V-sts, 2 sc in next ch-3 sp, rep from * around; join with sl st in beg sc. (42 sc)

Rnds 10–11: Ch 1, sc in same st as joining and in each st around; join with sl st in beg sc. (42 sc)

Rnd 12: Ch 3, dc in next st and in each st around; join with sl st in 3rd ch of beg ch-3. (42 dc)

Rnd 13: Ch 1, sc in same st as joining and in each st around; join with sl st in beg sc. (42 sc)

Fasten off. Weave in ends.

For button placement, follow the instructions at the end of the project.

Trendy Slouch Hat (3–6 months)

Ch 4; join with sl st in 1st ch to form ring.

Rnd 1: Ch 3 (counts as dc now and throughout), work 11 dc in ring; join with sl st in 3rd ch of beg ch-3 sp. (12 dc)

Rnd 2: Ch 3, dc in same st as joining, * 2 dc in next dc, rep from * around; join with sl st in 3rd ch of beg ch-3. (24 dc)

Rnd 3: Ch 3, 2 dc in next dc, * dc in next dc, 2 dc in next dc, rep from * around; join with sl st in 3rd ch of beg ch-3. (36 dc)

Rnd 4: Ch 3, dc in next 3 dc, 2 dc in next dc, * dc in next 4 dc, 2 dc in next dc, rep from * around to last st, dc in last st; join with sl st in 3rd ch of beg ch-3. (43 dc)

Rnd 5: Ch 2, hdc in next st and in each st around; join with sl st in 2nd ch of beg ch-2. (43 hdc)

Rnd 6: Ch 1, sc in same st as joining, * ch 2, sk next 2 hdc, sc in next hdc, rep from * around to last 3 sts, ch 2, sk next st, sc in next st, ch 2, sk last st; join with sl st in beg sc. (15 ch-2 sps)

Rnd 7: Ch 1, working in 1st ch-2 sp, sl st, ch 2 (yoh, insert hook in same ch-2 sp, draw up loop, yoh, pull yarn through 2 loops on hook) 2 times, yoh, draw through rem 3 loops on hook, ch 3, 3dc-cl in same ch-2 sp, ch 1, * (3dc-cl, ch 3, 3dc-cl, ch 1) in next ch-2 sp, rep from * around; join with sl st in beg 3dc-cl. (30 3dc-cl)

Rnd 8: Ch 1, (sl st, ch 7, tc) in 1st ch-3 sp, * (tc, ch 3, tc) (V-st made) in next ch-3 sp, rep from * around; join with sl st in 4th ch of beg ch-7. (15 V-sts)

Rnd 9: Ch 1, working in 1st ch-3 sp, sl st, ch 2 (yoh, insert hook in same ch-3 sp, draw up loop, yoh, pull yarn through 2 loops on hook) 2 times, yoh, draw through rem 3 loops on hook, ch 3, 3dc-cl in same ch-3 sp, ch 1, * (3dc-cl, ch 3, 3dc-cl, ch 1) in next ch-3 sp, rep from * around; join with sl st in beg 3dc-cl. (30 3dc-cl)

Rnds 10–11: Rep Rnds 8 and 9.

Rnd 12: Ch 1, (sl st, ch 1, 2 sc) in 1st ch-3 sp, * sc in next ch-1 sp, 2 sc in next ch-3 sp, rep from * around to last ch-1 sp, sc in last ch-1 sp; join with sl st in beg sc. (45 sc)

Rnds 13–14: Ch 1, sc in same st as joining and in each st around; join with sl st in beg sc. (45 sc)

Rnd 15: Ch 3, dc in next st and in each st around; join with sl st in 3rd ch of beg ch-3. (45 dc)

Rnd 16: Ch 1, sc in same st as joining and in each st around; join with sl st in beg sc. (45 sc)

Fasten off. Weave in ends.

For button placement, follow the instructions at the end of the project.

Trendy Slouch Hat *(6–12 months)*

Ch 4; join with sl st in 1st ch to form ring.

Rnd 1: Ch 3, work 11 dc in ring; join with sl st in 3rd ch of beg ch-3. (12 dc)

Rnd 2: Ch 3, dc in same st as joining, * 2 dc in next dc, rep from * around; join with sl st in 3rd ch of beg ch-3. (24 dc)

Rnd 3: Ch 3, 2 dc in next dc, * dc in next dc, 2 dc in next dc, rep from * around; join with sl st in 3rd ch of beg ch-3. (36 dc)

Rnd 4: Ch 3, dc in next dc, 2 dc in next dc, * dc in next 2 dc, 2 dc in next dc, rep from * around; join with sl st in 3rd ch of beg ch-3. (48 dc)

Rnd 5: Ch 2, hdc in next st and in each st around; join with sl st in 2nd ch of beg ch-2. (48 hdc)

Rnd 6: Ch 1, sc in same st as joining, * ch 2, sk next 2 hdc, sc in next hdc, rep from * around to last 2 sts, ch 2, sk last 2 sts; join with sl st in beg sc. (16 ch-2 sps)

Rnd 7: Ch 1, working in 1st ch-2 sp, sl st, ch 2, (yoh, insert hook in same ch-2 sp, draw up loop, yoh, pull yarn through 2 loops on hook) 2 times, yoh, draw through rem 3 loops on hook, ch 3, 3dc-cl in same ch-2 sp, ch 1, * (3dc-cl, ch 3, 3dc-cl, ch 1) in next ch-2 sp, rep from * around; join with sl st in beg 3dc-cl. (32 3dc-cl)

Rnd 8: Ch 1, (sl st, ch 7, tc) in 1st ch-3 sp, * (tc, ch 3, tc) (V-st made) in next ch-3 sp, rep from * around; join with sl st in 4th ch of beg ch-7. (16 V-sts)

Rnd 9: Ch 1, working in 1st ch-3 sp, sl st, ch 2, (yoh, insert hook in same ch-3 sp, draw up loop, yoh, pull yarn through 2 loops on hook) 2 times, yoh, draw through rem 3 loops on hook, ch 3, 3dc-cl in same ch-3 sp, ch 1, * (3dc-cl, ch 3, 3dc-cl, ch 1) in next ch-3 sp, rep from * around; join with sl st in beg 3dc-cl. (32 3dc-cl)

Rnds 10–12: Rep Rnds 8 and 9, ending on Rnd 8.

Rnd 13: Ch 1, sc in same st as joining, 2 sc in 1st ch-3 sp, * sc in ch st between 2 V-sts, 2 sc in next ch-3 sp, rep from * around; join with sl st in beg sc. (48 sc)

Rnds 14–15: Ch 1, sc in same st as joining and in each st around; join with sl st in beg sc. (48 sc)

Rnd 16: Ch 3, dc in next st and in each st around; join with sl st in 3rd ch of beg ch-3. (48 dc)

Rnd 17: Ch 1, sc in same st as joining and in each st around; join with sl st in beg sc. (48 sc)

Fasten off. Weave in ends.

For button placement, follow the instructions at the end of the project.

Trendy Slouch Hat *(1–3 years)*

Ch 4; join with sl st in 1st ch to form ring.

Rnd 1: Ch 3 (counts as dc now and throughout), work 11 dc in ring; join with sl st in 3rd ch of beg ch-3. (12 dc)

Rnd 2: Ch 3, dc in same st as joining, * 2 dc in next dc, rep from * around; join with sl st in 3rd ch of beg ch-3. (24 dc)

Rnd 3: Ch 3, 2 dc in next dc, * dc in next dc, 2 dc in next dc, rep from * around; join with sl st in 3rd ch of beg ch-3. (36 dc)

Rnd 4: Ch 3, dc in next dc, 2 dc in next dc, * dc in next 2 dc, 2 dc in next dc, rep from * around; join with sl st in 3rd ch of beg ch-3. (48 dc)

Rnd 5: Ch 2, hdc in next 7 dc, 2 hdc in next dc, * hdc in next 8 dc, 2 hdc in next dc, rep from * around to last 3 sts, hdc in last 3 sts; join with sl st in 2nd ch of beg ch-2. (53 hdc)

Rnds 6: Ch 1, sc in same st as joining, * ch 2, sk next 2 hdc, sc in next hdc, rep from * around to last st, ch 2, sk last st; join with sl st in beg sc. (18 ch-2 sps)

Rnd 7: Ch 1, working in 1st ch-2 sp, sl st, ch 2, (yoh, insert hook in same ch-2 sp, draw up loop, yoh, pull yarn through 2 loops on hook) 2 times, yoh, draw through rem 3 loops on hook, ch 3, 3dc-cl in same ch-2 sp, ch 1, * (3dc-cl, ch 3, 3dc-cl, ch 1) in next ch-2 sp, rep from * around; join with sl st in beg 3dc-cl. (36 3dc-cl)

Rnd 8: Ch 1, (sl st, ch 7, tc) in 1st ch-3 sp, * (tc, ch 3, tc) (V-st made) in next ch-3 sp, rep from * around; join with sl st in 4th ch of beg ch-7. (18 V-sts)

Rnd 9: Ch 1, working in 1st ch-3 sp, sl st, ch 2, (yoh, insert hook in same ch-3 sp, draw up loop, yoh, pull yarn through 2 loops on hook) 2 times yoh, draw through rem 3 loops on hook, ch 3, 3dc-cl in same ch-3 sp, ch 1, * (3dc-cl, ch 3, 3dc-cl, ch 1) in next ch-3 sp, rep from * around; join with sl st in beg 3dc-cl. (36 3dc-cl)

Rnds 10–13: Rep Rnds 8 and 9.

Rnd 14: Ch 1, (sl st, ch 1, 2 sc) in 1st ch-3 sp, * sc in next ch-1 sp, 2 sc in next ch-3 sp, rep from * around to last ch-1 sp, sc in last ch-1 sp; join with sl st in beg sc. (54 sc)

Rnds 15–16: Ch 1, sc in same st as joining and in each st around; join with sl st in beg sc. (54 sc)

Rnd 17: Ch 3, dc in next st and in each st around; join with sl st in 3rd ch of beg ch-3. (54 dc)

Rnd 18: Ch 1, sc in same st as joining and in each st around; join with sl st in beg sc. (54 sc)

Fasten off. Weave in ends.

For button placement, follow the instructions at the end of the project.

Trendy Slouch Hat *(4–8 years)*

Ch 4; join with sl st in 1st ch to form ring.

Rnd 1: Ch 3 (counts as dc now and throughout), work 11 dc in ring; join with sl st in 3rd ch of beg ch-3. (12 dc)

Rnd 2: Ch 3, dc in same st as joining, * 2 dc in next dc, rep from * around; join with sl st in 3rd ch of beg ch-3. (24 dc)

Rnd 3: Ch 3, 2 dc in next dc, * dc in next dc, 2 dc in next dc, rep from * around; join with sl st in 3rd ch of beg ch-3. (36 dc)

Rnd 4: Ch 3, dc in next dc, 2 dc in next dc, * dc in next 2 dc, 2 dc in next dc, rep from * around; join with sl st in 3rd ch of beg ch-3. (48 dc)

Rnd 5: Ch 3, dc in next 5 dc, 2 dc in next dc, * dc in next 6 dc, 2 dc in next dc, rep from * around to last 6 sts, dc in next 5 sts, 2 dc in last st; join with sl st in 3rd ch of beg ch-3. (55 dc)

Rnd 6: Ch 2, hdc in next st and in each st around, join with sl st in 2nd ch of beg ch-2. (55 hdc)

Rnd 7: Ch 1, sc in same st as joining, * ch 2, sk next 2 hdc, sc in next hdc, rep from * around to last 3 sts, ch 2, sk next st, sc in next st, ch 2, sk last st; join with sl st in beg sc. (19 ch-2 sps)

Rnd 8: Ch 1, working in 1st ch-2 sp, sl st, ch 2, (yoh, insert hook in same ch-2 sp, draw up loop, yoh, pull yarn through 2 loops on hook) 2 times, yoh, draw through rem 3 loops on hook, ch 3, 3dc-cl in same ch-2 sp, ch 1, * (3dc-cl, ch 3, 3dc-cl, ch 1) in next ch-2 sp, rep from * around; join with sl st in beg 3dc-cl. (38 3dc-cl)

Rnd 9: Ch 1, (sl st, ch 7, tc) in 1st ch-3 sp, * (tc, ch 3, tc) (V-st made) in next ch-3 sp, rep from * around; join with sl st in 4th ch of beg ch-7. (19 V-sts)

Rnd 10: Ch 1, working in 1st ch-3 sp, sl st, ch 2, (yoh, insert hook in same ch-3 sp, draw up loop, yoh, pull yarn through 2 loops on hook) 2 times, yoh, draw through rem 3 loops on hook, ch 3, 3dc-cl in same ch-3 sp, ch 1, * (3dc-cl, ch 3, 3dc-cl, ch 1) in next ch-3 sp, rep from * around; join with sl st in beg 3dc-cl. (38 3dc-cl)

Rnds 11–15: Rep Rnds 9 and 10, ending on Rnd 9.

Rnd 16: Ch 1, sc in same st as joining, 2 sc in 1st ch-3 sp, * sc in ch st between 2 V-sts, 2 sc in next ch-3 sp, rep from * around; join with sl st in beg sc. (57 sc)

Rnds 17–18: Ch 1, sc in same st as joining and in each st around; join with sl st in beg sc. (57 sc)

Rnd 19: Ch 3, dc in next st and in each st around; join with sl st in 3rd ch of beg ch-3. (57 dc)

Rnd 20: Ch 1, sc in same st as joining and in each st around; join with sl st in beg sc. (57 sc)

Fasten off. Weave in ends.

For button placement, follow the instructions at the end of the project.

Trendy Slouch Hat *(9 years–adult)*

Ch 4; join with sl st in 1st ch to form ring.

Rnd 1: Ch 3 (counts as dc now and throughout), work 11dc in ring; join with sl st in 3rd ch of beg ch-3. (12 dc)

Rnd 2: Ch 3, dc in same st as joining, * 2 dc in next dc, rep from * around; join with sl st in 3rd ch of beg ch-3. (24 dc)

Rnd 3: Ch 3, 2 dc in next dc, * dc in next dc, 2 dc in next dc, rep from * around; join with sl st in 3rd ch of beg ch-3. (36 dc)

Rnd 4: Ch 3, dc in next dc, 2 dc in next dc, * dc in next 2 dc, 2 dc in next dc, rep from * around; join with sl st in 3rd ch of beg ch-3. (48 dc)

Rnd 5: Ch 3, dc in next 3 dc, 2 dc in next dc, * dc in next 4 dc, 2 dc in next dc, rep from * around to last 3 sts, dc in next 2 sts, 2 dc in last st; join with sl st in 3rd ch of beg ch-3. (58 dc)

Rnd 6: Ch 3, dc in next st and in each st around; join with sl st in 3rd ch of beg ch-3. (58 dc)

Rnd 7: Ch 1, sc in same st as joining, * ch 2, sk next 2 dc, sc in next dc, rep from * around to last 3 sts, ch 2, sk next st, sc in next st, ch 2, sk last st; join with sl st in beg sc. (20 ch-2 sps)

Rnd 8: Ch 1, working in 1st ch-2 sp, sl st, ch 2, (yoh, insert hook in same ch-2 sp, draw up loop, yoh, pull yarn through 2 loops on hook) 2 times, yoh, draw through rem 3 loops on hook, ch 3, 3dc-cl in same ch-2 sp, ch 1, * (3dc-cl, ch 3, 3dc-cl, ch 1) in next ch-2 sp, rep from * around; join with sl st in beg 3dc-cl. (40 3dc-cl)

Rnd 9: Ch 1, (sl st, ch 7, tc) in 1st ch-3 sp, * (tc, ch 3, tc) (V-st made) in next ch-3 sp, rep from * around; join with sl st in 4th ch of beg ch-7. (20 V-sts)

Rnd 10: Ch 1, working in 1st ch-3 sp, sl st, ch 2, (yoh, insert hook in same ch-3 sp, draw up loop, yoh, pull yarn through 2 loops on hook) 2 times, yoh, draw through rem 3 loops on hook, ch 3, 3dc-cl in same ch-3 sp, ch 1, * (3dc-cl, ch 3, 3dc-cl, ch 1) in next ch-3 sp, rep from * around; join with sl st in beg 3dc-cl. (40 3dc-cl)

Rnds 11–16: Rep Rnds 9 and 10.

Rnd 17: Ch 1, (sl st, ch 1, 2 sc) in 1st ch-3 sp, * sc in next ch 1-sp, 2 sc in next ch-3 sp, rep from * around to last ch-1 sp, sc in last ch-1 sp; join with sl st in beg sc. (60 sc)

Rnds 18–19: Ch 1, sc in same st as joining and in each st around; join with sl st in beg sc. (60 sc)

Rnd 20: Ch 3, dc in next st and in each st around; join with sl st in 3rd ch of beg ch-3. (60 dc)

Rnd 21: Ch 1, sc in same st as joining and in each st around, join with sl st in beg sc. (60 sc)

Fasten off. Weave in ends.

For button placement, follow the instructions below.

Button Placement

With the joining seam of the hat facing you, sew the button onto the beg ch-3 of the double crochet round of the brim. To adjust the band for a perfect fit, simply pull any dc post to either side of the button and fold it over the button.

Newsboy Band Hat

Beep, beep, beep . . . the alarm clock sounds. Campbell and Tait jump out of bed, ecstatic because it's Sunday morning and they get to go fishing with their dad! Just as they are about to leave the house, they change the bands on the Newsboy Hats that I made for them. They never leave home without them because good things always happen, including catching "the big one," while they have their lucky hats on!

MATERIALS

For Newsboy Band Hat: Light sport weight yarn **(3)** in the color of your choice

- 0–3 mos. (100yd/91.4m)
- 3–6 mos. (110yd/100.6m)
- 6–12 mos. (130yd/118.9m)
- 1–3 yrs. (150yd/137.2m)
- 4–8 yrs. (160yd/146.3m)
- 9 yrs.–adult (180yd/164.6m)

For Newsboy Brim: Light sport weight yarn in the same color as the hat (18yd/16.5m)

Size I (5.5mm) crochet hook

$\frac{7}{8}$"–1" (2.2cm–2.5cm) button

Tapestry needle

Scissors

Finished Project Sizes

To fit approx. 0–3 months: 12"–13½" (30.5cm–34.3cm) circumference

To fit approx. 3–6 months: 14"–15" (35.6cm–38.1cm) circumference

To fit approx. 6–12 months: 15"–16½" (38.1cm–41.9cm) circumference

To fit approx. 1–3 years: 16½"–18" (41.9cm–45.7cm) circumference

To fit approx. 4–8 years: 18½"–20" (47cm–50.8cm) circumference

To fit approx. 9 years–adult: 20½"–22" (52.1cm–55.9cm) circumference

Gauge

15 sts = 4" (10.2m);
7 rows dc = 4" (10.2cm)

Glossary of Abbreviations

ch(s)	chain(s)
st(s)	stitch(s)
sl st	slip stitch
sp(s)	space(s)
beg	beginning
rep	repeat
rnd(s)	round(s)
sc	single crochet
hdc	half double crochet
dc	double crochet
*	repeat instructions following the asterisk as directed.

Newsboy Band Hat (0–3 months)

Ch 4; join with sl st in 1st ch to form ring.

Rnd 1: Ch 3 (counts as dc now and throughout), work 11 dc in ring; join with sl st in 3rd ch of beg ch-3. (12 dc)

Rnd 2: Ch 3, dc in same st as joining, * 2 dc in next dc, rep from * around; join with sl st in 3rd ch of beg ch-3. (24 dc)

Rnd 3: Ch 3, 2 dc in next 2 dc, * dc in next dc, 2 dc in next 2 dc, rep from * around; join with sl st in 3rd ch of beg ch-3. (40 dc)

Rnds 4–9: Ch 3, dc in next st and in each st around; join with sl st in 3rd ch of beg ch-3. (40 dc)

Rnd 10: Ch 2, hdc in next st and in each st around; join with sl st in 2nd ch of beg ch-2. (40 hdc)

Snug Rnd (this round prevents the brim of the hat from stretching): Ch 1, sc in same st as joining, sl st in next 2 hdc, * sc in next hdc, sl st in next 2 hdc, rep from * around to last st, sc in last st; join with sl st in beg sc. (40 sts)

Fasten off. Weave in ends.

For instructions on button placement and creating the interchangeable band, see the end of the project.

To add the Newsboy Brim, see the end of the chapter.

Newsboy Band Hat (3–6 months)

Ch 4; join with sl st in 1st ch to form ring.

Rnd 1: Ch 3 (counts as dc now and throughout), work 11 dc in ring; join with sl st in 3rd ch of beg ch-3. (12 dc)

Rnd 2: Ch 3, dc in same st as joining, * 2 dc in next dc, rep from * around; join with sl st in 3rd ch of beg ch-3. (24 dc)

Rnd 3: Ch 3, 2 dc in next dc, * dc in next dc, 2 dc in next dc, rep from * around; join with sl st in 3rd ch of beg ch-3. (36 dc)

Rnd 4: Ch 3, dc in next 3 dc, 2 dc in next dc, * dc in next 4 dc, 2 dc in next dc, rep from * around to last st, dc in last st; join with sl st in 3rd ch of beg ch-3. (43 dc)

Rnds 5–10: Ch 3, dc in next st and in each st around; join with sl st in 3rd ch of beg ch-3. (43 dc)

Rnd 11: Ch 2, hdc in next st and in each st around; join with sl st in 2nd ch of beg ch-2. (43 hdc)

Snug Rnd (this round prevents the brim of the hat from stretching): Ch 1, sc in same st as joining, sl st in next 2 hdc, * sc in next hdc, sl st in next 2 hdc, rep from * around to last st, sc in last st; join with sl st in beg sc. (43 sts)

Fasten off. Weave in ends.

For instructions on button placement and creating the interchangeable band, see the end of the project.

To add the Newsboy Brim, see the end of the chapter.

Newsboy Band Hat *(6–12 months)*

Ch 4; join with sl st in 1st ch to form ring.

Rnd 1: Ch 3 (counts as dc now and throughout), work 11 dc in ring; join with sl st in 3rd ch of beg ch-3. (12 dc)

Rnd 2: Ch 3, dc in same st as joining, * 2 dc in next dc, rep from * around; join with sl st in 3rd ch of beg ch-3. (24 dc)

Rnd 3: Ch 3, 2 dc in next dc, * dc in next dc, 2 dc in next dc, rep from * around; join with sl st in 3rd ch of beg ch-3. (36 dc)

Rnd 4: Ch 3, dc in next dc, 2 dc in next dc, * dc in next 2 dc, 2 dc in next dc, rep from * around; join with sl st in 3rd ch of beg ch-3. (48 dc)

Rnds 5–11: Ch 3, dc in next st and in each st around; join with sl st in 3rd ch of beg ch-3. (48 dc)

Rnd 12: Ch 2, hdc in next st and in each st around; join with sl st in 2nd ch of beg ch-2. (48 hdc)

Snug Rnd (this round prevents the brim of the hat from stretching): Ch 1, sc in same st as joining, sl st in next 2 hdc, * sc in next hdc, sl st in next 2 hdc, rep from * around; join with sl st in beg sc. (48 sts)

Fasten off. Weave in ends.

For instructions on button placement and creating the interchangeable band, see the end of the project.

To add the Newsboy Brim, see the end of the chapter.

Newsboy Band Hat *(1–3 years)*

Ch 4; join with sl st in 1st ch to form ring.

Rnd 1: Ch 3 (counts as dc now and throughout), work 11 dc in ring; join with sl st in 3rd ch of beg ch-3. (12 dc)

Rnd 2: Ch 3, dc in same st as joining, * 2 dc in next dc, rep from * around; join with sl st in 3rd ch of beg ch-3. (24 dc)

Rnd 3: Ch 3, 2 dc in next dc, * dc in next dc, 2 dc in next dc, rep from * around; join with sl st in 3rd ch of beg ch-3. (36 dc)

Rnd 4: Ch 3, dc in next dc, 2 dc in next dc, * dc in next 2 dc, 2 dc in next dc, rep from * around; join with sl st in 3rd ch of beg ch-3. (48 dc)

Rnd 5: Ch 3, dc in next 7 sts, 2 dc in next dc, * dc in next 8 dc, 2 dc in next dc, rep from * around to last 3 sts, dc in last 3 sts; join with sl st in 3rd ch of beg ch-3. (53 dc)

Rnds 6–12: Ch 3, dc in next st and in each st around; join with sl st in 3rd ch of beg ch-3. (53 dc)

Rnd 13: Ch 2, hdc in next st and in each st around; join with sl st in 2nd ch of beg ch-2. (53 hdc)

Snug Rnd (this round prevents the brim of the hat from stretching): Ch 1, sc in same st as joining, sl st in next 2 hdc, * sc in next hdc, sl st in next 2 hdc, rep from * around to last 2 sts, sc in next st, sl st in last st; join with sl st in beg sc. (53 sts)

Fasten off. Weave in ends.

For instructions on button placement and creating the interchangeable band, see the end of the project.

To add the Newsboy Brim, see the end of the chapter.

Newsboy Band Hat *(4–8 years)*

Ch 4; join with sl st in 1st ch to form ring.

Rnd 1: Ch 3 (counts as dc now and throughout), work 11 dc in ring; join with sl st in 3rd ch of beg ch-3. (12 dc)

Rnd 2: Ch 3, dc in same st as joining, * 2 dc in next dc, rep from * around; join with sl st in 3rd ch of beg ch-3. (24 dc)

Rnd 3: Ch 3, 2 dc in next dc, * dc in next dc, 2 dc in next dc, rep from * around; join with sl st in 3rd ch of beg ch-3. (36 dc)

Rnd 4: Ch 3, dc in next dc, 2 dc in next dc, * dc in next 2 dc, 2 dc in next dc, rep from * around; join with sl st in 3rd ch of beg ch-3. (48 dc)

Rnd 5: Ch 3, dc in next 5 dc, 2 dc in next dc, * dc in next 6 dc, 2 dc in next dc, rep from * around to last 6 sts, dc in next 5 sts, 2 dc in last st; join with sl st in 3rd ch of beg ch-3. (55 dc)

Rnds 6–13: Ch 3, dc in next st and in each st around; join with sl st in 3rd ch of beg ch-3. (55 dc)

Rnd 14: Ch 2, hdc in next st and in each st around, join with sl st in 2nd ch of beg ch-2. (55 hdc)

Snug Rnd (this round prevents the brim of the hat from stretching): Ch 1, sc in same st as joining, sl st in next 2 hdc, * sc in next hdc, sl st in next 2 hdc, rep from * around to last st, sc in last st; join with sl st in beg sc. (55 st)

Fasten off. Weave in ends.

For instructions on button placement and creating the interchangeable band, see the end of the project.

To add the Newsboy Brim, see the end of the chapter.

Newsboy Band Hat *(9 years–adult)*

Ch 4; join with sl st in 1st ch to form ring.

Rnd 1: Ch 3 (counts as dc now and throughout), work 11 dc in ring; join with sl st in 3rd ch of beg ch-3. (12 dc)

Rnd 2: Ch 3, dc in same st as joining, * 2 dc in next dc, rep from * around; join with sl st in 3rd ch of beg ch-3. (24 dc)

Rnd 3: Ch 3, 2 dc in next dc, * dc in next dc, 2 dc in next dc, rep from * around; join with sl st in 3rd ch of beg ch-3. (36 dc)

Rnd 4: Ch 3, dc in next dc, 2 dc in next dc, * dc in next 2 dc, 2 dc in next dc, rep from * around; join with sl st in 3rd ch of beg ch-3. (48 dc)

Rnd 5: Ch 3, dc in next 3 dc, 2 dc in next dc, * dc in next 4 dc, 2 dc in next dc, rep from * around to last 3 sts, dc in next 2 sts, 2 dc in last st; join with sl st in 3rd ch of beg ch-3. (58 dc)

Rnds 6–14: Ch 3, dc in next st and in each st around; join with sl st in 3rd ch of beg ch-3. (58 dc)

Rnd 15: Ch 2, hdc in next st and in each st around; join with sl st in 2nd ch of beg ch-2. (58 hdc)

Snug Rnd (this round prevents the brim of hat from stretching): Ch 1, sc in same st as joining, sl st in next 2 hdc, * sc in next hdc, sl st in next 2 hdc, rep from * around to last st, sc in last st; join with sl st in beg sc. (58 sts)

Fasten off. Weave in ends.

For instructions on button placement and creating the interchangeable band, see the end of the project.

To add the Newsboy Brim, see the end of the chapter.

Button Placement

Once the Newsboy Brim has been added to the hat, sew one button onto the 2nd dc rnd up from each corner of the Newsboy Brim.

Button the interchangeable band onto the buttons using the 3 hdc holes on each side of band. **Note:** If the band is for the 0–3 month hat size, you may have to button the band through one of the end dc to make the band fit snugly.

Sew a big, chunky wooden button on this hat or add an interchangeable motif to change the look for a boy or a girl. Add some color with stripes or make the hat without the brim for a simple, stylish beanie. (see the Stitches & Techniques section for information about color changes.)

Make an Interchangeable Band

With I hook and yarn color of your choice, ch 22.

Row 1: Dc in 4th ch from hook and in each ch to end. (20 dc)

Rnd 2: Do not turn; ch 2, work 3 hdc inside the ending dc sp, 2 hdc in next st, hdc in next 18 sts, 2 hdc in next st, work 3 hdc inside the ending dc sp, 2 hdc in next dc, hdc in next 18 dc, then hdc in the ch-st between hdc just made and the beg ch 2, sl st in 2nd ch of beg ch-2. (50 hdc)

Fasten off. Weave in ends.

Twisted Headband

I can see it now: An adorable little flower girl walking down the aisle wearing this precious headband with a flower motif made to match the bridesmaids' dresses. It's breathtaking. These super-quick headbands make perfect last-minute gifts. They are adjustable for a perfect fit and can be made in any color under the rainbow. Make them for all your family and friends, from newborns to adults.

MATERIALS

For Twisted Headband: Light sport weight yarn (3) in the color of your choice

- 0–3 mos. (36yd/32.9m)
- 3–6 mos. (40yd/36.6m)
- 6–12 mos. (45yd/41.1m)
- 1–3 yrs. (56yd/51.2m)
- 4–8 yrs. (62yd/56.7m)
- 9 yrs.–adult (65yd/59.4m)

Size I (5.5mm) crochet hook

1⅛" (2.8cm) button

Tapestry needle

Scissors

Finished Project Sizes

To fit approx. 0–3 months: 12"–13½" (30.5cm–34.3cm) circumference

To fit approx. 3–6 months: 14"–15" (35.6cm–38.1cm) circumference

To fit approx. 6–12 months: 15"–16½" (38.1cm–41.9cm) circumference

To fit approx. 1–3 years: 16½"–18" (41.9cm–45.7cm) circumference

To fit approx. 4–8 years: 18½"–20" (47cm–50.8cm) circumference

To fit approx. 9 years–adult: 20½"–22" (52.1cm–55.9cm) circumference

Gauge

15 sts = 4" (10.2cm);
7 rows dc = 4" (10.2cm)

Glossary of Abbreviations

ch(s)	chain(s)
st(s)	stitch(es)
sl st	slip stitch
sp(s)	space(s)
beg	beginning
sk	skip
rep	repeat
bpdc	back post double crochet
hdc	half double crochet
dc	double crochet
PS	puff stitch
*	repeat instructions following the asterisk as directed
()	work instructions within the parentheses as many times as directed

For instructions on how to do a Puff Stitch and a Back Post Double Crochet (bpdc), see Stitches & Techniques.

Note: If you use a larger size button (that fits between the headband stitches) than what the pattern calls for, you will need to adjust the center ring size of the interchangeable motifs so they fit over the button. You can do this by simply chaining more stitches for the beginning loop.

Twisted Headband *(0–3 months)*

Ch 46.

Row 1: Hdc in 3rd ch from hook and in each ch across. (45 hdc)

Row 2 (Puff Stitch Row): Turn, ch 3, PS in next hdc, * sk next 2 hdc, (dc, ch 2, PS) in next hdc, rep from * to last st, dc in last st. (15 PS)

Row 3: Turn, ch 2, 3 hdc in next ch-2 sp. Work 1 bpdc around the post of the next unworked hdc in Row 1, * 2 hdc in next ch-2 sp, work 1 bpdc around the post of the next unworked hdc in Row 1, rep from * to end; then hdc in 2nd ch of the ending ch-3 sp. (45 sts)

Snug Rnd (this round prevents the headband from stretching): Do not turn. Ch 1, sl st in same st as last hdc and in each st around all 4 sides of the headband; join with sl st to beg sl st.

Fasten off. Weave in ends.

Sew a 1⅛" (2.8cm) button onto the end of the puffed-up side of the headband.

To fasten headband (adjust): Button into any hole on the headband, then place the motif of your choice over the button.

Twisted Headband (3–6 months)

Ch 51.

Row 1: Hdc in 3rd ch from hook and in each ch across. (50 hdc)

Row 2 (Puff Stitch Row): Turn, ch 3, PS in next hdc, * sk next 2 hdc, (dc, ch 2, PS) in next hdc, rep from * to last 3 sts, sk next 2 sts, dc in last st. (16 PS)

Row 3: Turn, ch 2, 3 hdc in next ch-2 sp. Work 1 bpdc around the post of the next unworked hdc in Row 1, * 2 hdc in next ch-2 sp, work 1 bpdc around the post of the next unworked hdc in Row 1, rep from * to end; next work 2 hdc in ending ch-3 sp, then hdc in 2nd ch of the same ch-3 sp. (50 sts)

Snug Rnd (this round prevents the headband from stretching): Do not turn. Ch 1, sl st in same st as last hdc and in each st around all 4 sides of the headband; join with sl st to beg sl st.

Fasten off. Weave in ends.

Sew a 1⅛" (2.8m) button onto the end of the puffed-up side of the headband.

To fasten headband (adjust): Button into any hole on the headband, then place the motif of your choice over the button.

Twisted Headband (6–12 months)

Ch 56.

Row 1: Hdc in 3rd ch from hook and in each ch across. (55 hdc)

Row 2 (Puff Stitch Row): Turn, ch 3, PS in next hdc, * sk next 2 hdc, (dc, ch 2, PS) in next hdc, rep from * to last 2 sts, sk next st, dc in last st. (18 PS)

Row 3: Turn, ch 2, 3 hdc in next ch-2 sp. Work 1 bpdc around the post of the next unworked hdc in Row 1, * 2 hdc in next ch-2 sp, work 1 bpdc around the post of the next unworked hdc in Row 1, rep from * to end; next work 1 hdc in ending ch-3 sp, then hdc in 2nd ch of the same ch-3 sp. (55 sts)

Snug Rnd (this round prevents the headband from stretching): Do not turn. Ch 1, sl st in same st as last hdc and in each st around all 4 sides of the headband; join with sl st to beg sl st.

Fasten off. Weave in ends.

Sew a 1⅛" (2.8cm) button onto the end of the puffed-up side of the headband.

To fasten headband (adjust): Button into any hole on the headband, then place the motif of your choice over the button.

Twisted Headband *(1–3 years)*

Ch 61.

Row 1: Hdc in 3rd ch from hook and in each ch across. (60 hdc)

Row 2 (Puff Stitch Row): Turn, ch 3, PS in next hdc, * sk next 2 hdc, (dc, ch 2, PS) in next hdc, rep from * to last st, dc in last st. (20 PS)

Row 3: Turn, ch 2, 3 hdc in next ch-2 sp. Work 1 bpdc around the post of the next unworked hdc in Row 1, * 2 hdc in next ch-2 sp, work 1 bpdc around the post of the next unworked hdc in Row 1, rep from * to end; then hdc in 2nd ch of the ending ch-3 sp. (60 sts)

Snug Rnd (this round prevents the headband from stretching): Do not turn. Ch 1, sl st in same st as last hdc and in each st around all 4 sides of the headband; join with sl st to beg sl st.

Fasten off. Weave in ends.

Sew a 1⅛" (2.8cm) button onto the end of the puffed-up side of the headband.

To fasten headband (adjust): Button into any hole on the headband, then place the motif of your choice over the button.

Twisted Headband *(4–8 years)*

Ch 66.

Row 1: Hdc in 3rd ch from hook and in each ch across. (65 hdc)

Row 2 (Puff Stitch Row): Turn, ch 3, PS in next hdc, * sk next 2 hdc, (dc, ch 2, PS) in next hdc, rep from * to last 3 sts, sk next 2 sts, dc in in last st. (21 PS)

Row 3: Turn, ch 2, 3 hdc in next ch-2 sp. Work 1 bpdc around the post of the next unworked hdc in Row 1, * 2 hdc in next ch-2 sp, work 1 bpdc around the post of the next unworked hdc in Row 1, rep from * to end, next work 2 hdc in the ending ch-3 sp, then hdc in 2nd ch of the same ch-3 sp. (65 sts)

Snug Rnd (this round prevents the headband from stretching): Do not turn. Ch 1, sl st in same st as last hdc and in each st around all 4 sides of the headband; join with sl st to beg sl st.

Fasten off. Weave in ends.

Sew a 1⅛" (2.8cm) button onto the end of the puffed-up side of the headband.

To fasten headband (adjust): Button into any hole on the headband, then place the motif of your choice over the button.

Twisted Headband *(9 years–adult)*

Ch 71.

Row 1: Hdc in 3rd ch from hook and in each ch across. (70 hdc)

Row 2 (Puff Stitch Row): Turn, ch 3, PS in next hdc, * sk next 2 hdc, (dc, ch 2, PS) in next hdc, rep from * to last 2 sts, sk next st, dc in last st. (23 PS)

Row 3: Turn, ch 2, 3 hdc in next ch-2 sp. Work 1 bpdc around the post of the next unworked hdc in Row 1, * 2 hdc in next ch-2 sp, work 1 bpdc around the post of the next unworked hdc in Row 1, rep from * to end; next work 1 hdc in the ending ch-3 sp, then hdc in 2nd ch of the same ch-3 sp. (70 sts)

Snug Round (this round prevents the headband from stretching): Do not turn. Ch 1, sl st in same st as last hdc and in each st around all 4 sides of the headband; join with sl st to beg sl st.

Fasten off. Weave in ends.

Sew a 1⅛" (2.8cm) button onto the end of the puffed-up side of the headband.

To fasten headband (adjust): Button into any hole on the headband, then place the motif of your choice over the button.

Multifunctional Hair Ties

BEGINNER

A sweet little flower is all your little flower needs to think of you during the day. When I was little, I loved colorful, fun hair ties (and still do). Now you can create your own hair treasures. Try wearing it across your forehead for a chic "boho" look, or even as a choker necklace with a Pinwheel Posy made using that yarn you've been saving for something special. Make the ties longer for a trendy belt, or tie them onto your bag or backpack so you can tell it apart from the others. Change them into friendship bracelets or anklets by making them shorter. What a great little project to do on a rainy day. They're great stash-busters too! Play around with different yarns, from self-striping to funky fibers, to give each one its own look.

MATERIALS

For Hair Ties: Light sport weight yarn 〔3〕 in the color of your choice

Size I (5.5mm) crochet hook

1⅛" (2.8cm) button

Tapestry needle

Scissors

Finished Project Sizes

One size

Gauge

No gauge required

Glossary of Abbreviations

ch(s)	chain(s)
sc	single crochet
dc	double crochet

Multi-Functional Hair Ties

Ch 100.

Row 1: Sc in 2nd ch from hook, sc in next 32 ch, dc in next 33 ch, sc in last 33 ch. (99 sts)

Fasten off. Weave in ends.

Sew a button onto the 17th dc.

Button on your favorite interchangeable motif from Chapter 2.

Serena Beanie

I used basic stitches and a simple pattern to create this elegant hat. Top it off with a big, chunky wooden button or crochet a motif in a luxurious yarn. You can also add more rows to the body to make a fabulous slouch hat. This is the perfect addition to a dress-up or a dress-down kind of day.

MATERIALS

For Serena Beanie: Light sport weight yarn 🧶3🧶 in the color of your choice:

- 0–3 mos. (80yd/73.2m)
- 3–6 mos. (90yd/82.3m)
- 6–12 mos. (100yd/91.4m)
- 1–3 yrs. (110yd/100.6m)
- 4–8 yrs. (120yd/109.7m)
- 9 yrs.–adult (130yd/118.9m)

Size I (5.5mm) crochet hook

Size J (6mm) crochet hook

⅞"–1" (2.2cm–2.5cm) button

Tapestry needle

Scissors

Finished Project Sizes

To fit approx. 0–3 months: 12"–13½" (30.5cm–34.3cm) circumference

To fit approx. 3–6 months: 14"–15" (35.6cm–38.1cm) circumference

To fit approx. 6–12 months: 15"–16½" (38.1cm–41.9cm) circumference

To fit approx. 1–3 years: 16½"–18" (41.9cm–45.7cm) circumference

To fit approx. 4–8 years: 18½"–20" (47cm–50.8cm) circumference

To fit approx. 9 years–adult: 20½"–22" (52.1cm–55.9cm) circumference

Gauge

15 st = 4" (10.2cm); 7 rows hdc = 4" (10.2cm)

Glossary of Abbreviations

ch(s)   chain(s)
st(s)   stitch(s)
sl st   slip stitch
beg   beginning
rep   repeat
rnd(s) round(s)
sc   single crochet
hdc   half double crochet
tc   treble crochet
*   repeat instructions following the asterisk as directed

Serena Beanie *(0–3 months)*

With I (5.5mm) hook, ch 4; join with sl st in 1st ch to form ring.

Rnd 1: Ch 2 (counts as hdc now and throughout), work 11 hdc in ring; join with sl st in 2nd ch of beg ch-2. (12 hdc)

Rnd 2: Ch 2, hdc in same st as joining, * 2 hdc in next hdc; rep from * around; join with sl st in 2nd ch of beg ch-2. (24 hdc)

Rnd 3: Ch 2, 2 hdc in next 2 hdc, * hdc in next hdc, 2 hdc in next 2 hdc, rep from * around; join with sl st in 2nd ch of beg ch-2. (40 hdc)

Switch to J (6mm) hook.

Rnd 4: Ch 4 (counts as tc), sc in next hdc, * tc in next hdc, sc in next hdc, rep from * around; join with sl st in 4th ch of beg ch-4. (40 sts)

Rnd 5: Ch 1, sc in same st as joining, tc in next sc, * sc in next tc, tc in next sc, rep from * around; join with sl st in beg sc. (40 sts)

Rnd 6: Ch 4, sc in next tc, * tc in next sc, sc in next tc, rep from * around; join with sl st in 4th ch of beg ch-4. (40 sts)

Rnds 7–11: Rep Rnds 5 and 6, ending on Rnd 5.

Switch to I (5.5mm) hook.

Rnds 12–15: Ch 1, sc in same st as joining and in each st around; join with sl st in beg sc. (40 sc)

Fasten off. Weave in ends.

For instructions on button placement, see the end of the project.

Serena Beanie *(3–6 months)*

With I hook, ch 4; join with sl st in 1st ch to form ring.

Rnd 1: Ch 2 (counts as hdc now and throughout), work 11 hdc in ring; join with sl st in 2nd ch of beg ch-2. (12 hdc)

Rnd 2: Ch 2, hdc in same st as joining, * 2 hdc in next hdc; rep from * around; join with sl st in 2nd ch of beg ch-2. (24 hdc)

Rnd 3: Ch 2, 2 hdc in next hdc, * hdc in next hdc, 2 hdc in next hdc; rep from * around; join with sl st in 2nd ch of beg ch-2. (36 hdc)

Rnd 4: Ch 2, hdc in same st as joining, hdc in next 3 hdc, 2 hdc in next hdc, * hdc in next 4 hdc, 2 hdc in next hdc, rep from * around to last hdc, hdc in last hdc; join with sl st in 2nd ch of beg ch-2. (44 hdc)

Switch to J (6mm) hook.

Rnd 5: Ch 4 (counts as tc), sc in next hdc, * tc in next hdc, sc in next hdc, rep from * around, join with sl st in 4th ch of beg ch-4. (44 sts)

Rnd 6: Ch 1, sc in same st as joining, tc in next sc, * sc in next tc, tc in next sc, rep from * around; join with sl st in beg sc. (44 sts)

Rnd 7: Ch 4, sc in next tc, * tc in next tc, sc in next tc, rep from * around; join with sl st in 4th ch of beg ch-4. (44 sts)

Rnds 8–12: Rep Rnds 6 and 7, ending on Rnd 6.

Switch to I (5.5mm) hook.

Rnds 13–16: Ch 1, sc in same st as joining and in each st around, join with sl st in beg sc. (44 sc)

Fasten off. Weave in ends.

For instructions on button placement, see the end of the project.

Serena Beanie *(6–12 months)*

With I (5.5mm) hook, ch 4; join with sl st in 1st ch to form ring.

Rnd 1: Ch 2 (counts as hdc now and throughout), work 11 hdc in ring; join with sl st in 2nd ch of beg ch-2. (12 hdc)

Rnd 2: Ch 2, hdc in same st as joining, * 2 hdc in next hdc, rep from * around; join with sl st in 2nd ch of beg ch-2. (24 hdc)

Rnd 3: Ch 2, 2 hdc in next hdc, * hdc in next hdc, 2 hdc in next hdc, rep from * around; join with sl st in 2nd ch of beg ch-2. (36 hdc)

Rnd 4: Ch 2, hdc in next hdc, 2 hdc in next hdc, * hdc in next 2 hdc, 2 hdc in next hdc, rep from * around; join with sl st in 2nd ch of beg ch-2. (48 hdc)

Switch to J (6mm) hook.

Rnd 5: Ch 4 (counts as tc), sc in next hdc, * tc in next hdc, sc in next hdc, rep from * around; join with sl st in 4th ch of beg ch-4. (48 sts)

Rnd 6: Ch 1, sc in same st as joining, tc in next sc, * sc in next tc, tc in next sc, rep from * around; join with sl st in beg sc. (48 sts)

Rnd 7: Ch 4, sc in next tc, * tc in next sc, sc in next tc, rep from * around; join with sl st in 4th ch of beg ch-4. (48 sts)

Rnds 8–14: Rep Rnds 6 and 7, ending on Rnd 6.

Switch to I (5.5mm) hook.

Rnds 15–18: Ch 1, sc in same st as joining and in each st around; join with sl st in beg sc. (48 sc)

Fasten off. Weave in ends.

For instructions on button placement, see the end of the project.

Serena Beanie *(1–3 years)*

With I (5.5mm) hook, ch 4; join with sl st in 1st ch to form ring.

Rnd 1: Ch 2 (counts as hdc now and throughout), work 11 hdc in ring; join with sl st in 2nd ch of beg ch-2. (12 hdc)

Rnd 2: Ch 2, hdc in same st as joining, * 2 hdc in next hdc, rep from * around; join with sl st in 2nd ch of beg ch-2. (24 hdc)

Rnd 3: Ch 2, 2 hdc in next hdc, * hdc in next hdc, 2 hdc in next hdc, rep from * around; join with sl st in 2nd ch of beg ch-2. (36 hdc)

Rnd 4: Ch 2, hdc in next hdc, 2 hdc in next hdc, * hdc in next 2 hdc, 2 hdc in next hdc, rep from * around; join with sl st in 2nd ch of beg ch-2. (48 hdc)

Rnd 5: Ch 2, hdc in next 10 hdc, 2 hdc in next hdc, * hdc in next 11 hdc, 2 hdc in next hdc, rep from * around; join with sl st in 2nd ch of beg ch-2. (52 hdc)

Switch to J (6mm) hook.

Rnd 6: Ch 4 (counts as tc), sc in next hdc, * tc in next hdc, sc in next hdc, rep from * around; join with sl st in 4th ch of beg ch-4. (52 sts)

Rnd 7: Ch 1, sc in same st as joining, tc in next sc, * sc in next tc, tc in next sc, rep from * around; join with sl st in beg sc. (52 sts)

Rnd 8: Ch 4, sc in next tc, * tc in next sc, sc in next tc, rep from * around; join with sl st in 4th ch of beg ch-4. (52 sts)

Rnds 9–16: Rep Rnds 7 and 8.

Switch to I (5.5mm) hook.

Rnds 17–21: Ch 1, sc in same st as joining and in each st around; join with sl st in beg sc. (52 sc)

Fasten off. Weave in ends.

For instructions on button placement, see the end of the project.

Serena Beanie *(4–8 years)*

With I hook, ch 4; join with sl st in 1st ch to form ring.

Rnd 1: Ch 2 (counts as hdc now and throughout), work 11 hdc in ring; join with sl st in 2nd ch of beg ch-2. (12 hdc)

Rnd 2: Ch 2, hdc in same st as joining, * 2 hdc in next hdc, rep from * around; join with sl st in 2nd ch of beg ch-2. (24 hdc)

Rnd 3: Ch 2, 2 hdc in next hdc, * hdc in next hdc, 2 hdc in next hdc, rep from * around; join with sl st in 2nd ch of beg ch-2. (36 hdc)

Rnd 4: Ch 2, hdc in next hdc, 2 hdc in next hdc, * hdc in next 2 hdc, 2 hdc in next hdc, rep from * around; join with sl st in 2nd ch of beg ch-2. (48 hdc)

Rnd 5: Ch 2, hdc in next 4 hdc, 2 hdc in next hdc, * hdc in next 5 hdc, 2 hdc in next hdc, rep from * around; join with sl st in 2nd ch of beg ch-2. (56 hdc)

Switch to J (6mm) hook.

Rnd 6: Ch 4 (counts as tc), sc in next hdc, * tc in next hdc, sc in next hdc, rep from * around; join with sl st in 4th ch of beg ch-4. (56 sts)

Rnd 7: Ch 1, sc in same st as joining, tc in next sc, * sc in next tc, tc in next sc, rep from * around; join with sl st in beg sc. (56 sts)

Rnd 8: Ch 4, sc in next tc, * tc in next sc, sc in next tc, rep from * around; join with sl st in 4th ch of beg ch-4. (56 sts)

Rnds 9–17: Rep Rnds 7 and 8, ending on Rnd 7.

Switch to I (5.5mm) hook.

Rnds 18–22: Ch 1, sc in same st as joining and in each st around; join with sl st in beg sc. (56 sc)

Fasten off. Weave in ends.

For instructions on button placement, see the end of the project.

Serena Beanie (9 years–adult)

With I (5.5mm) hook, ch 4; join with sl st in 1st ch to form ring.

Rnd 1: Ch 2 (counts as hdc now and throughout), work 11 hdc in ring; join with sl st in 2nd ch of beg ch-2. (12 hdc)

Rnd 2: Ch 2, hdc in same st as joining, * 2 hdc in next hdc, rep from * around; join with sl st in 2nd ch of beg ch-2. (24 hdc)

Rnd 3: Ch 2, 2 hdc in next hdc, * hdc in next hdc, 2 hdc in next hdc, rep from * around; join with sl st in 2nd ch of beg ch-2. (36 hdc)

Rnd 4: Ch 2, hdc in next hdc, 2 hdc in next hdc, * hdc in next 2 hdc, 2 hdc in next hdc, rep from * around; join with sl st in 2nd ch of beg ch-2. (48 hdc)

Rnd 5: Ch 2, hdc in next 2 hdc, 2 hdc in next hdc, * hdc in next 3 hdc, 2 hdc in next hdc, rep from * around; join with sl st in 2nd ch of beg ch-2. (60 hdc)

Switch to J (6mm) hook.

Rnd 6: Ch 4 (counts as tc), sc in next hdc, * tc in next hdc, sc in next hdc, rep from * around; join with sl st in 4th ch of beg ch-4. (60 sts)

Rnd 7: Ch 1, sc in same st as joining, tc in next sc, * sc in next tc, tc in next sc, rep from * around; join with sl st in beg sc. (60 sts)

Rnd 8: Ch 4, sc in next tc, * tc in next sc, sc in next tc, rep from * around; join with sl st in 4th ch of beg ch-4. (60 sts)

Rnds 9–18: Rep Rnds 7 and 8.

Switch to I (5.5mm) hook.

Rnds 19–24: Ch 1, sc in same st as joining and in each st around; join with sl st in beg sc. (60 sc)

Fasten off. Weave in ends.

For instructions on button placement, see the information below.

> ## Button Placement:
>
> Sew a button 1"–1½" (2.5cm–3.8cm) from the bottom of the brim on the side of your choice. Attach your favorite motif from Chapter 2.

Comfy Cloche

This is the perfect hat for the colder months. Whip some up for your family and friends in their favorite colors and add bright, interchangeable flowers. They're sure to fall in love with them!

MATERIALS

For Comfy Cloche: Worsted weight yarn ⟨4⟩ in the color of your choice

- 0–3 mos. (75yd/68.6m)
- 3–6 mos. (80yd/73.2m)
- 6–12 mos. (85yd/77.7m)
- 1–3 yrs. (90yd/82.3m)
- 4–8 yrs. (95yd/86.9m)
- 9 yrs.–adult (100yd/91.4m)

Size J (6mm) crochet hook

⅞"–1" (2.2cm–2.5cm) button

Tapestry needle

Scissors

Finished Project Sizes

To fit approx. 0-3 months: 12"–13½" (30.5cm–34.3cm) circumference

To fit approx. 3-6 months: 14"–15" (35.6cm–38.1cm) circumference

To fit approx. 6-12 months: 15"–16½" (38.1cm–41.9cm) circumference

To fit approx. 1-3 years: 16½"–18" (41.9cm–45.7cm) circumference

To fit approx. 4-8 years: 18½"–20" (47cm–50.8cm) circumference

To fit approx. 9 years–adult: 20½"–22" (52.1cm–55.9cm) circumference

Gauge

15 st = 4" (10.2cm);
7 rows dc = 4" (10.2cm)

Glossary of Abbreviations

ch(s)	chain(s)
st(s)	stitch(s)
sl st	slip stitch
beg	beginning
rep	repeat
rnd(s)	round(s)
sc	single crochet
hdc	half double crochet
dc	double crochet
*	repeat instructions following the asterisk as directed

Comfy Cloche (0–3 months)

Ch 4; join with sl st in 1st ch to form ring.

Rnd 1: Ch 1, work 9 sc in ring; join with sl st in beg sc. (9 sc)

Rnd 2: Ch 2, hdc in same st as joining, * 2 hdc in next sc, rep from * around; join with sl st in 2nd ch of beg ch-2. (18 hdc)

Rnd 3: Ch 3 (counts as dc now and throughout), dc in next hdc, * 2 dc in next hdc, dc in next hdc, rep from * around to end, then dc in ch st between the last dc just made and the beg ch-3; join with sl st in the 3rd ch of the beg ch-3. (27 dc)

Rnd 4: Ch 3, dc in next 2 dc, * 2 dc in next dc, dc in next 2 dc, rep from * around to end, then dc in ch st between the last dc just made and the beg ch-3; join with sl st in the 3rd ch of the beg ch-3. (36 dc)

Rnds 5–7: Ch 3, dc in next st and in each st around; join with sl st in 3rd ch of beg ch-3. (36 dc)

Rnd 8: Ch 2, hdc in same st as joining and in each st around; join with sl st in 2nd ch of beg ch-2. (37 hdc)

Rnd 9: Ch 1, sc in same st as joining and in each st around; join with sl st in beg sc. (37 sc)

Rnd 10: Ch 1, sc in same st as joining, sc in next sc, * 2 sc in next sc, sc in next 4 sc, rep from * around; join with sl st in beg sc. (44 sc)

Rnd 11: Ch 1, sc in same st as joining, 2 sc in next sc, * sc in next sc, rep from * around; join with sl st in beg sc. (45 sc)

Rnd 12: Ch 1, sc in same st as joining and in each st around; join with sl st in beg sc. (45 sc)

Rnd 13: Ch 1, 2 sc in same st as joining, * sc in next sc, rep from * around; join with sl st in beg sc. (46 sc)

Fasten off. Weave in ends.

For instructions on button placement, see the end of the project.

Comfy Cloche *(3–6 months)*

Ch 4; join with sl st in 1st ch to form ring.

Rnd 1: Ch 1, work 9 sc in ring; join with sl st in beg sc. (9 sc)

Rnd 2: Ch 2, hdc in same st as joining, * 2 hdc in next sc, rep from * around; join with sl st in 2nd ch of beg ch-2. (18 hdc)

Rnd 3: Ch 3 (counts as dc now and throughout), dc in next hdc, * 2 dc in next hdc, dc in next hdc, rep from * around to end, then dc in ch st between the last dc just made and the beg ch-3; join with sl st in the 3rd ch of the beg ch-3. (27 dc)

Rnd 4: Ch 3, dc in next 2 dc, * 2 dc in next dc, dc in next 2 dc, rep from * around to end, then dc in ch st between the last dc just made and the beg ch-3; join with sl st in the 3rd ch of the beg ch-3. (36 dc)

Rnd 5: Ch 3, dc in next 11 dc, * 2 dc in next dc, dc in next 11 dc, rep from * around to end, then dc in ch st between the last dc just made and the beg ch-3; join with sl st in the 3rd ch of the beg ch-3. (39 dc)

Rnds 6–8: Ch 3, dc in next st and in each st around; join with sl st in 3rd ch of beg ch-3. (39 dc)

Rnd 9: Ch 2, hdc in same st as joining and in each st around; join with sl st in 2nd ch of beg ch-2. (40 hdc)

Rnd 10: Ch 1, sc in same st as joining and in each st around; join with sl st in beg sc. (40 sc)

Rnd 11: Ch 1, sc in same st as joining, sc in next 2 sc, 2 sc in next sc, * sc in next 5 sc, 2 sc in next sc, rep from * around; join with sl st in beg sc. (47 sc)

Rnd 12: Ch 1, sc in same st as joining, 2 sc in next sc, * sc in next sc, rep from * around; join with sl st in beg sc. (48 sc)

Rnds 13–14: Ch 1, sc in same st as joining and in each st around; join with sl st in beg sc. (48 sc)

Rnds 15: Ch 1, 2 sc in same st as joining, * sc in next sc, rep from * around; join with sl st in beg sc. (49 sc)

Fasten off. Weave in ends.

For instructions on button placement, see the end of the project.

Comfy Cloche (6–12 months)

Ch 4; join with sl st in 1st ch to form ring.

Rnd 1: Ch 1, work 9 sc in ring; join with sl st in beg sc. (9 sc)

Rnd 2: Ch 2, hdc in same st as joining, * 2 hdc in next sc, rep from * around; join with sl st in 2nd ch of beg ch-2. (18 hdc)

Rnd 3: Ch 3 (counts as dc now and throughout), dc in next hdc, * 2 dc in next hdc, dc in next hdc, rep from * around to end, then dc in ch st between the last dc just made and the beg ch-3; join with sl st in the 3rd ch of the beg ch-3. (27 dc)

Rnd 4: Ch 3, dc in next 2 dc, * 2 dc in next dc, dc in next 2 dc, rep from * around to end, then dc in ch st between the last dc just made and the beg ch-3; join with sl st in the 3rd ch of the beg ch-3. (36 dc)

Rnd 5: Ch 3, dc in next 5 dc, * 2 dc in next dc, dc in next 5 dc, rep from * around to end, then dc in ch st between the last dc just made and the beg ch-3; join with sl st in the 3rd ch of the beg ch-3. (42 dc)

Rnds 6–8: Ch 3, dc in next st and in each st around; join with sl st in 3rd ch of beg ch-3. (42 dc)

Rnd 9: Ch 2, hdc in same st as joining and in each st around, join with sl st in 2nd ch of beg ch-2. (43 hdc)

Rnd 10: Ch 1, sc in same st as joining and in each st around;,join with sl st in beg sc. (43 sc)

Rnd 11: Ch 1, 2 sc in same st as joining, * sc in next 6 sc, 2 sc in next sc, rep from * around; join with sl st in beg sc. (50 sc)

Rnd 12: Ch 1, sc in same st as joining, 2 sc in next sc, * sc in next sc, rep from * around; join with sl st in beg sc. (51 sc)

Rnds 13–15: Ch 1, sc in same st as joining and in each st around; join with sl st in beg sc. (51 sc)

Rnd 16: Ch 1, 2 sc in same st as joining, * sc in next sc, rep from * around; join with sl st in beg sc. (52 sc)

Fasten off. Weave in ends.

For instructions on button placement, see the end of the project.

Comfy Cloche (1–3 years)

Ch 4; join with sl st in 1st ch to form ring.

Rnd 1: Ch 1, work 9 sc in ring; join with sl st in beg sc. (9 sc)

Rnd 2: Ch 2, hdc in same st as joining, * 2 hdc in next sc, rep from * around; join with sl st in 2nd ch of beg ch-2. (18 hdc)

Rnd 3: Ch 3 (counts as dc now and throughout), dc in next hdc, * 2 dc in next hdc, dc in next hdc, rep from * around to end, then dc in ch st between the last dc just made and the beg ch-3; join with sl st in the 3rd ch of the beg ch-3. (27 dc)

Rnd 4: Ch 3, dc in next 2 dc, * 2 dc in next dc, dc in next 2 dc, rep from * around to end, then dc in ch st between the last dc just made and the beg ch-3; join with sl st in the 3rd ch of the beg ch-3. (36 dc)

Rnd 5: Ch 3, dc in next 5 dc, * 2 dc in next dc, dc in next 2 dc, rep from * around to end, then dc in ch st between the last dc just made and the beg ch-3; join with sl st in the 3rd ch of the beg ch-3. (47 dc)

Rnds 6–9: Ch 3, dc in next st and in each st around; join with sl st in 3rd ch of beg ch-3. (47 dc)

Rnd 10: Ch 2, hdc in same st as joining and in each st around; join with sl st in 2nd ch of beg ch-2. (48 hdc)

Rnd 11: Ch 1, sc in same st as joining and in each st around; join with sl st in beg sc. (48 sc)

Rnd 12: Ch 1, sc in same st as joining, sc in next sc, 2 sc in next sc, * sc in next 4 sc, 2 sc in next sc, rep from * around; join with sl st in beg sc. (58 sc)

Rnd 13: Ch 1, sc in same st as joining, 2 sc in next sc, * sc in next sc, rep from * around; join with sl st in beg sc. (59 sc)

Rnds 14–16: Ch 1, sc in same st as joining and in each st around; join with sl st in beg sc. (59 sc)

Rnd 17: Ch 1, 2 sc in same st as joining, * sc in next sc, rep from * around; join with sl st in beg sc. (60 sc)

Fasten off. Weave in ends.

For instructions on button placement, see the end of the project.

Comfy Cloche (4–8 years)

Ch 4; join with sl st in 1st ch to form ring.

Rnd 1: Ch 1, work 9 sc in ring; join with sl st in beg sc. (9 sc)

Rnd 2: Ch 2, hdc in same st as joining, * 2 hdc in next sc, rep from * around; join with sl st in 2nd ch of beg ch-2. (18 hdc)

Rnd 3: Ch 3 (counts as dc now and throughout), dc in next hdc, * 2 dc in next hdc, dc in next hdc, rep from * around to end, then dc in ch st between the last dc just made and the beg ch-3; join with sl st in the 3rd ch of the beg ch-3. (27 dc)

Rnd 4: Ch 3, dc in next 2 dc, * 2 dc in next dc, dc in next 2 dc, rep from * around to end, then dc in ch st between the last dc just made and the beg ch-3; join with sl st in the 3rd ch of the beg ch-3. (36 dc)

Rnd 5: Ch 3, dc in next 3 dc, * 2 dc in next dc, dc in next 3 dc, rep from * around to end, then dc in ch st between the last dc just made and the beg ch-3; join with sl st in the 3rd ch of the beg ch-3. (45 dc)

Rnd 6: Ch 3, dc in next 8 dc, * 2 dc in next dc, dc in next 8 dc, rep from * around to end, then dc in ch st between the last dc just made and the beg ch-3; join with sl st in the 3rd ch of the beg ch-3. (50 dc)

Rnds 7–10: Ch 3, dc in next st and in each st around; join with sl st in 3rd ch of beg ch-3. (50 dc)

Rnd 11: Ch 2, hdc in same st as joining and in each st around; join with sl st in 2nd ch of beg ch-2. (51 hdc)

Rnd 12: Ch 1, sc in same st as joining and in each st around; join with sl st in beg sc. (51 sc)

Rnd 13: Ch 1, sc in same st as joining, sc in next 4 sc, 2 sc in next sc, * sc in next 4 sc, 2 sc in next sc, rep from * around; join with sl st in beg sc. (61 sc)

Rnd 14: Ch 1, sc in same st as joining, 2 sc in next sc, * sc in next sc, rep from * around; join with sl st in beg sc. (62 sc)

Rnds 15–17: Ch 1, sc in same st as joining and in each st around; join with sl st in beg sc. (62 sc)

Rnd 18: Ch 1, 2 sc in same st as joining, 2 sc in next sc, * sc in next sc, rep from * around; join with sl st in beg sc. (64 sc)

Fasten off. Weave in ends.

For instructions on button placement, see the end of the project.

Comfy Cloche *(9 years–adult)*

Ch 4; join with sl st in 1st ch to form ring.

Rnd 1: Ch 1, work 9 sc in ring; join with sl st in beg sc. (9 sc)

Rnd 2: Ch 2, hdc in same st as joining, * 2 hdc in next sc, rep from * around; join with sl st in 2nd ch of beg ch-2. (18 hdc)

Rnd 3: Ch 3 (counts as dc now and throughout), dc in next hdc, * 2 dc in next hdc, dc in next hdc, rep from * around to end, then dc in ch st between the last dc just made and the beg ch-3; join with sl st in the 3rd ch of the beg ch-3. (27 dc)

Rnd 4: Ch 3, dc in next 2 dc, * 2 dc in next dc, dc in next 2 dc, rep from * around to end, then dc in ch st between the last dc just made and the beg ch-3; join with sl st in the 3rd ch of the beg ch-3. (36 dc)

Rnd 5: Ch 3, dc in next 3 dc, * 2 dc in next dc, dc in next 3 dc, rep from * around to end, then dc in ch st between the last dc just made and the beg ch-3; join with sl st in the 3rd ch of the beg ch-3. (45 dc)

Rnd 6: Ch 3, dc in next 4 dc, * 2 dc in next dc, dc in next 4 dc, rep from * around to end, then dc in ch st between the last dc just made and the beg ch-3; join with sl st in the 3rd ch of the beg ch-3. (54 dc)

Rnds 7–10: Ch 3, dc in next st and in each st around; join with sl st in 3rd ch of beg ch-3. (54 dc)

Rnd 11: Ch 2, hdc in same st as joining and in each st around; join with sl st in 2nd ch of beg ch-2. (55 hdc)

Rnd 12: Ch 1, sc in same st as joining and in each st around; join with sl st in beg sc. (55 sc)

Rnd 13: Ch 1, sc in same st as joining, sc in next 3 sc, 2 sc in next sc, * sc in next 4 sc, 2 sc in next sc, rep from * around; join with sl st in beg sc. (66 sc)

Rnd 14: Ch 1, sc in same st as joining, 2 sc in next sc, * sc in next sc, rep from * around; join with sl st in beg sc. (67 sc)

Rnds 15–18: Ch 1, sc in same st as joining and in each st around; join with sl st in beg sc. (67 sc)

Rnd 19: Ch 1, 2 sc in same st as joining, 2 sc in next sc, * sc in next sc, rep from * around; join with sl st in beg sc. (69 sc)

Fasten off. Weave in ends.

For instructions on button placement, see information below.

Button Placement

Orient the joining seam toward the back and sew a button 1"–1½" (2.5cm–3.8cm) from the bottom of the brim on the side of your choice.

Adjustable Ribbed Head Wrap

These head wraps are a definite must-have for those cold days. They are stylish and adjustable to provide the perfect fit. Not into head wraps? Whip one up anyway and wear it as a neck wrap! You can leave the pattern the way it is or continue the pattern to make it wider. Coordinate the colors of the neck wrap and the motif to match your warm coat. You will be the talk of the town!

MATERIALS

For Head Wrap Option #1: 2 strands of light sport weight yarn ⟨3⟩ in the color of your choice for a 3¼"-wide to 4¼"-wide (8.3cm–10.8cm) head wrap

For Head Wrap Option #2: 1 strand of worsted weight yarn ⟨4⟩ in the color of your choice for a 3¼"-wide to 4¼"-wide (8.3cm–10.8cm) head wrap.

- 0–3 mos. (100–130yd/91.4–118.9m)
- 3–6 mos. (110–140yd/100.6–128m)
- 6–12 mos. (120–150yd/109.7–137.2m)
- 1–3 yrs. (130–160yd/118.9–146.3m)
- 4–8 yrs. (140–170yd/128–155.4m)
- 9 yrs.–adult (150–180yd/138–165m)

Size I (5.5mm) crochet hook

Five ⅞" (2.2cm) buttons (only four needed for 3¼"-wide [8.3cm] wrap)

Tapestry needle

Scissors

Finished Project Sizes

To fit approx. 0–3 months: 12"–13½" (30.5cm–34.3cm) circumference

To fit approx. 3–6 months: 14"–15" (35.6cm–38.1cm) circumference

To fit approx. 6–12 months: 15"–16½" (38.1cm–41.9cm) circumference

To fit approx. 1–3 years: 16½"–18" (41.9cm–45.7cm) circumference

To fit approx. 4–8 years: 18½"–20" (47cm–50.8cm) circumference

To fit approx. 9 years–adult: 20½"–22" (52.1cm–55.9cm) circumference

Gauge

No gauge required.

Glossary of Abbreviations

ch(s)   chain(s)
st(s)   stitch(s)
sl st   slip stitch
beg   beginning
rep   repeat
rnd(s)   round(s)
hdc   half double crochet
fphdc   front post half double crochet
bphdc   back post half double crochet
*   repeat instructions following the asterisk as directed

Adjustable Ribbed Head Wrap *(0–3 months)*

With 2 strands of sport weight yarn or 1 strand of worsted weight yarn, ch 50.

Row 1: Hdc in 3rd ch from hook, hdc in each ch across. (49 hdc)

Row 2: Turn, ch 2 (counts as hdc now and throughout), * fphdc around next hdc, rep from * across to last st, hdc in last st. (49 hdc)

Row 3: Turn, ch 2, * bphdc around next hdc, rep from * across to last st, hdc in last st. (49 hdc)

Row 4: Turn, ch 2, hdc in next st and in each st across. (49 hdc)

Row 5: Turn, ch 2, * bphdc around next hdc, rep from * across to last st, hdc in last st. (49 hdc)

Row 6: Turn, ch 2, * fphdc around next hdc, rep from * across to last st, hdc in last st. (49 hdc)

Row 7: Turn, ch 2, hdc in next st and in each st across. (49 hdc)

Rows 8–9: Rep Rows 2 and 3.

Rnd 10: Do not fasten off. Do not turn. Ch 1, sl st in each st around the head wrap; join with sl st in beg ch-1.

Fasten off. Weave in ends.

Finishing the Head Wrap

On one edge of the head wrap, sew a button in the middle of each raised ridge (3 buttons). This row of buttons will be placed behind the head or neck (if you are using it as a neck wrap). Fold the other end over and button through the opposite raised ridge holes of your choice to obtain a perfect fit. Sew the remaining button onto the side of the head wrap and button on your favorite motif.

Adjustable Ribbed Head Wrap *(3–6 months)*

With 2 strands of sport weight yarn or 1 strand of worsted weight yarn, ch 55.

Row 1: Hdc in 3rd ch from hook, hdc in each ch across. (54 hdc)

Row 2: Turn, ch 2 (counts as hdc now and throughout), * fphdc around next hdc, rep from * across to last st, hdc in last st. (54 hdc)

Row 3: Turn, ch 2, * bphdc around next hdc, rep from * across to last st, hdc in last st. (54 hdc)

Row 4: Turn, ch 2, hdc in next st and in each st across. (54 hdc)

Row 5: Turn, ch 2, * bphdc around next hdc, rep from * across to last st, hdc in last st. (54 hdc)

Row 6: Turn, ch 2, * fphdc around next hdc, rep from * across to last st, hdc in last st. (54 hdc)

Row 7: Turn, ch 2, hdc in next st and in each st across. (54 hdc)

Rows 8–9: Rep Rows 2 and 3.

Rnd 10: Do not fasten off. Do not turn. Ch 1, sl st in each st around the head wrap; join with sl st in beg ch-1.

Fasten off. Weave in ends.

Finishing the Head Wrap

On one edge of the head wrap, sew a button in the middle of each raised ridge (3 buttons). This row of buttons will be placed behind the head or neck (if you are using it as a neck wrap). Fold the other end over and button through the opposite raised ridge holes of your choice to obtain a perfect fit. Sew the remaining button onto the side of the head wrap and button on your favorite motif.

Adjustable Ribbed Head Wrap *(6–12 months)*

With 2 strands of sport weight yarn or 1 strand of worsted weight yarn, ch 60.

Row 1: Hdc in 3rd ch from hook, hdc in each ch across. (59 hdc)

Row 2: Turn, ch 2 (counts as hdc now and throughout), * fphdc around next hdc, rep from * across to last st, hdc in last st. (59 hdc)

Row 3: Turn, ch 2, * bphdc around next hdc, rep from * across to last st, hdc in last st. (59 hdc)

Row 4: Turn, ch 2, hdc in next st and in each st across. (59 hdc)

Row 5: Turn, ch 2, * bphdc around next hdc, rep from * across to last st, hdc in last st. (59 hdc)

Row 6: Turn, ch 2, * fphdc around next hdc, rep from * across to last st, hdc in last st. (59 hdc)

Row 7: Turn, ch 2, hdc in next st and in each st across. (59 hdc)

Rows 8–9: Rep Rows 2 and 3.

To make the 3¼"-wide (8.3cm) head wrap, proceed with Rnd 1 for the 3¼"-wide (8.3cm) head wrap.

To make the 4¼"-wide (10.8cm) head wrap, continue with Row 10.

Rows 10–12: Rep Rows 4–6.

Proceed with Rnd 1 for the 4¼"-wide (10.8cm) head wrap.

Rnd 1 for the 3¼"-wide (8.3cm) head wrap: Do not fasten off. Do not turn. Ch 1, sl st in each st around the head wrap; join with sl st in beg ch-1.

Fasten off. Weave in ends.

Rnd 1 for the 4¼"-wide (10.8cm) head wrap: Do not fasten off. Turn, ch 1, sl st in each st around the head wrap; join with sl st in beg ch-1.

Fasten off. Weave in ends.

Finishing the Head Wrap

On one edge of the head wrap, sew a button in the middle of each raised ridge (3 buttons for the 3¼"-wide [8.3cm] head wrap, 4 buttons for the 4¼"-wide [10.8cm] head wrap). This row of buttons will be placed behind the head or neck (if you are using it as a neck wrap). Fold the other end over and button through the opposite raised ridge holes of your choice to obtain a perfect fit. Sew the remaining button onto the side of the head wrap and button on your favorite motif.

Adjustable Ribbed Head Wrap (1–3 years)

With 2 strands of sport weight yarn or 1 strand of worsted weight yarn, ch 65.

Row 1: Hdc in 3rd ch from hook, hdc in each ch across. (64 hdc)

Row 2: Turn, ch 2 (counts as hdc now and through-out), * fphdc around next hdc, rep from * across to last st, hdc in last st. (64 hdc)

Row 3: Turn, ch 2, * bphdc around next hdc, rep from * across to last st, hdc in last st. (64 hdc)

Row 4: Turn, ch 2, hdc in next st and in each st across. (64 hdc)

Row 5: Turn, ch 2, * bphdc around next hdc, rep from * across to last st, hdc in last st. (64 hdc)

Row 6: Turn, ch 2, * fphdc around next hdc, rep from * across to last st, hdc in last st. (64 hdc)

Row 7: Turn, ch 2, hdc in next st and in each st across. (64 hdc)

Rows 8–9: Rep Rows 2 and 3.

To make the 3¼"-wide (8.3cm) head wrap, proceed with Rnd 1 for the 3¼"-wide (8.3cm) head wrap.

To make the 4¼"-wide (10.8cm) head wrap, continue with Row 10.

Rows 10–12: Rep Rows 4–6.

Proceed with Rnd 1 for the 4¼"-wide (10.8cm) head wrap.

Rnd 1 for the 3¼"-wide (8.3cm) head wrap: Do not fasten off. Do not turn. Ch 1, sl st in each st around the head wrap; join with sl st in beg ch-1.

Fasten off. Weave in ends.

Rnd 1 for the 4¼"-wide (10.8cm) head wrap: Do not fasten off. Turn, ch 1, sl st in each st around the head wrap; join with sl st in beg ch-1.

Fasten off. Weave in ends.

Finishing the Head Wrap

On one edge of the head wrap, sew a button in the middle of each raised ridge (3 buttons for the 3¼"-wide [8.3cm] head wrap, 4 buttons for the 4¼"-wide [10.8cm] head wrap). This row of buttons will be placed behind the head or neck (if you are using it as a neck wrap). Fold the other end over and button through the opposite raised ridge holes of your choice to obtain a perfect fit. Sew the remaining button onto the side of the head wrap and button on your favorite motif.

Adjustable Ribbed Head Wrap *(4–8 years)*

With 2 strands of sport weight yarn or 1 strand of worsted weight yarn, ch 70.

Row 1: Hdc in 3rd ch from hook, hdc in each ch across. (69 hdc)

Row 2: Turn, ch 2 (counts as hdc now and throughout), * fphdc around next hdc, rep from * across to last st, hdc in last st. (69 hdc)

Row 3: Turn, ch 2, * bphdc around next hdc, rep from * across to last st, hdc in last st. (69 hdc)

Row 4: Turn, ch 2, hdc in next st and in each st across. (69 hdc)

Row 5: Turn, ch 2, * bphdc around next hdc, rep from * across to last st, hdc in last st. (69 hdc)

Row 6: Turn, ch 2, * fphdc around next hdc, rep from * across to last st, hdc in last st. (69 hdc)

Row 7: Turn, ch 2, hdc in next st and in each st across. (69 hdc)

Rows 8–9: Rep Rows 2 and 3.

To make the 3¼"-wide (8.3cm) head wrap, proceed with Rnd 1 for the 3¼"-wide (8.3cm) head wrap.

To make the 4¼"-wide (10.8cm) head wrap, continue with Row 10.

Rows 10–12: Rep Rows 4–6.

Proceed with Rnd 1 for the 4¼"-wide (10.8cm) head wrap.

Rnd 1 for the 3¼"-wide (8.3cm) head wrap: Do not fasten off. Do not turn. Ch 1, sl st in each st around the head wrap; join with sl st in beg ch-1.

Fasten off. Weave in ends.

Rnd 1 for the 4¼"-wide (10.8cm) head wrap: Do not fasten off. Turn, ch 1, sl st in each st around the head wrap; join with sl st in beg ch-1.

Fasten off. Weave in ends.

Finishing the Head Wrap

On one edge of the head wrap, sew a button in the middle of each raised ridge (3 buttons for the 3¼"-wide [8.3cm] head wrap, 4 buttons for the 4¼"-wide [10.8cm] head wrap). This row of buttons will be placed behind the head or neck (if you are using it as a neck wrap). Fold the other end over and button through the opposite raised ridge holes of your choice to obtain a perfect fit. Sew the remaining button onto the side of the head wrap and button on your favorite motif.

Adjustable Ribbed Head Wrap (9 years-adult)

With 2 strands of sport weight yarn or 1 strand of worsted weight yarn, ch 75.

Row 1: Hdc in 3rd ch from hook, hdc in each ch across. (74 hdc)

Row 2: Turn, ch 2 (counts as hdc now and throughout), * fphdc around next hdc, rep from * across to last st, hdc in last st. (74 hdc)

Row 3: : Turn, ch 2, * bphdc around next hdc, rep from * across to last st, hdc in last st. (74 hdc)

Row 4: Turn, ch 2, hdc in next st and in each st across. (74 hdc)

Row 5: Turn, ch 2, * bphdc around next hdc, rep from * across to last st, hdc in last st. (74 hdc)

Row 6: Turn, ch 2, * fphdc around next hdc, rep from * across to last st, hdc in last st. (74 hdc)

Row 7: Turn, ch 2, hdc in next st and in each st across. (74 hdc)

Rows 8–9: Rep Rows 2 and 3.

To make the 3¼"-wide (8.3cm) head wrap, proceed with Rnd 1 for the 3¼"-wide (8.3cm) head wrap.

To make the 4¼"-wide (10.8cm) head wrap, continue with Row 10.

Rows 10–12: Rep Rows 4–6.

Proceed with Rnd 1 for the 4¼"-wide (10.8cm) head wrap.

Rnd 1 for the 3¼"-wide (8.3cm) head wrap: Do not fasten off. Do not turn. Ch 1, sl st in each st around the head wrap; join with sl st in beg ch-1.

Fasten off. Weave in ends.

Rnd 1 for the 4¼"-wide (10.8cm) head wrap: Do not fasten off. Turn, ch 1, sl st in each st around the head wrap; join with sl st in beg ch-1.

Fasten off. Weave in ends.

Finishing the Head Wrap

On one edge of the head wrap, sew one button in the middle of each raised ridge (3 buttons for the 3¼"-wide [8.3cm] head wrap, 4 buttons for the 4¼"-wide [10.8cm] head wrap). This row of buttons will be placed behind the head or neck (if you are using it as a neck wrap). Fold the other end over and button through the opposite raised ridge holes of your choice to obtain a perfect fit. Sew the remaining button onto the side of the head wrap and button on your favorite motif.

Button Placement and Optional Brims

Button Placement

For the Beanie

Make sure the joining seam of the hat is facing the back. Sew the button 1"–1½" (2.5cm–3.8cm) from the bottom of the brim on one side. Attach the motif of your choice to the button.

For the Newsboy Brim

Sew the button 1"–1½" (2.5cm–3.8cm) up from one edge of the newsboy brim.

For the Sunhat Brim

Make sure the joining seam of the hat is toward the back. As a guide, fold the Sunhat Brim up to touch the hat. Sew the button on the hat behind the dc round (Rnd 1) of the Sunhat Brim on the side of your choice. Once the button is sewn on, push the button through the dc round of the brim.

Add a Sunhat Brim

Hat Placement

Orient the hat with the top of the hat facing you and the last joining stitch facing up (in the middle).

All Sizes:

Position the hat as directed above. Using two strands of sport weight yarn, insert the hook in the chain space to the right of the joining stitch. Join the yarn.

Rnd 1: Ch 3 (counts as dc now and throughout), 5 dc in same ch sp, dc in sc, * 6 dc in next ch sp, dc in sc, rep from * around; join with sl st in 3rd ch of beg ch-3.

Rnd 2: Ch 2, hdc in each dc around; join with sl st in 2nd ch of beg ch-2.

Fasten off. Weave in ends.

Add a Newsboy Brim

Hat Placement

Orient the top of the hat so it faces you with the joining seam on the right side.

Make the Newsboy Brim
(0–3 months / 3–6 months / 6–12 months)

For the Twisted Beanie & Newsboy Band Hat:
You will be working Row 1 and the ending sl sts in the hdc rnd before the Snug Rnd.

For the Scalloped Beanie: You will be working Row 1 and the ending sl sts in the last sc rnd of the beanie.

Position the hat as directed under Hat Placement. Using two strands of sport weight yarn, insert the hook in the 6th st to the right of the upper left corner and join yarn.

Row 1: Ch 1, insert hook in same st and draw up a loop, yoh, insert hook in next st, draw up a loop, yoh, draw through all 4 loops on hook (dec made), (2 dc in next st, dc in next st) 6 times, yoh, insert hook in next st and draw up loop, yoh, insert hook in next st and draw up loop, yoh and draw through all 5 loops on hook (dec made). (20 sts)

Row 2: Ch 1, turn, sk next st, insert hook in next dc, draw up loop, yoh, insert hook in next dc and draw up loop, yoh and draw through all 4 loops on hook (dec made), * 2 hdc in next dc, hdc in next 2 dc, rep from * to last 5 sts, 2 hdc in next dc, hdc in next dc, yoh, insert hook in next dc and draw up loop, yoh, insert hook in next st and draw up loop, yoh, draw through all 5 loops on hook (dec made), sl st in last st, then sl st in st beside the Row 1 beg st. (23 sts)

Row 3: Ch 1, turn, sk next st, sl st in next st and in each st until end of row, then sl st in st beside the Row 1 dec st.

Make the Newsboy Brim
(1–3 years / 4–8 years / 9 years–adult)

For the Twisted Beanie & Newsboy Band Hat:
You will be working Row 1 and the ending sl sts in the hdc rnd before the Snug Rnd.

For the Scalloped Beanie: You will be working Row 1 and the ending sl sts in the last sc rnd of the beanie.

Position the hat as directed under Hat Placement. Using two strands of sport weight yarn, insert the hook in the 8th st to the right of the upper left corner and join yarn.

Row 1: Ch 1, insert hook in same st and draw up loop, yoh, insert hook in next st, draw up loop, yoh, draw through all 4 loops on hook (dec made), (2 dc in next st, dc in next st) 7 times, yoh, insert hook in next st and draw up loop, yoh, insert hook in next st and draw up loop, yoh and draw through all 5 loops on hook (dec made). (23 sts)

Row 2: Ch 1, turn, sk next st, insert hook in next dc, draw up loop, yoh, insert hook in next dc and draw up loop, yoh and draw through all 4 loops on hook (dec made), * 2 dc in next dc, dc in next 2 dc, rep from * to last 5 sts, 2 dc in next dc, dc in next dc, yoh, insert hook in next dc and draw up loop, yoh, insert hook in next dc and draw up loop, yoh, draw through all 5 loops on hook (dec made), sl st in last st, then sl st in st beside the Row 1 beg st. (27 sts)

Row 3: Ch 1, turn, sk next st, sl st in next st and in each st until end of row, then sl st in st beside the Row 1 dec st.

Chapter 2
Interchangeable Flowers & Motifs

Let your creativity shine while making these fun flowers and motifs! Each one uses only a small amount of yarn, so they make great stash busters. Feel free to break the rules and pull out those wild and funky fibers, scrap pieces and embellishments to create these motifs. After you've finished one, you'll want to make them all!

Want to use a different size button than the pattern calls for? Simply adjust the center ring of the motif by increasing or decreasing the amount of chains to form the beginning loop. This simple alteration will make it fit over the button.

Not only can you change the look of any of the projects in this book by adding these embellishments in different colors, textures or fibers, but you can create with them in many other ways, too!

P.S. Little girls *love* these accents! They get to pick whichever flower or motif their little hearts desire. Better yet, they get to put it on themselves!

Triple-Tier Clusters

These flowers make the perfect finishing touch for a handbag, sweater or accessory. For instance, add a pin to the back and make a beautiful brooch! Once you've learned the pattern, try using a highly textured yarn to give them extra dimension and pop.

MATERIALS

Light sport weight yarn in the color of your choice

Size I (5.5mm) crochet hook

Tapestry needle

Scissors

Finished Project Size

Approx. 4" (10.2cm) across

Gauge

No gauge required.

This flower is worked in rounds. Turn it when indicated to work in the back of the flower.

Glossary of Abbreviations

ch(s)   chain(s)
st(s)   stitch(s)
sl st   slip stitch
sp(s)   space(s)
beg   beginning
rep   repeat
sc   single crochet
hdc   half double crochet
dc   double crochet
*   repeat instructions following the asterisk as directed
( )   work instructions within the brackets as many times as directed

Make the Triple-Tier Clusters

Ch 5; join with sl st in beg ch to form a ring.

Rnd 1: Ch 1, sc in ring, (ch 3, sc in ring) 5 times, ch 3; join with sl st in beg sc. (6 ch-3 sps)

Rnd 2: Ch 1, * (sc, hdc, 3 dc, hdc, sc) in next ch-3 sp, rep from * around; join with sl st in beg sc. (6 petals)

Rnd 3: Ch 1, turn (working behind Rnd 2), sl st in same st as joining sl st, * (ch 3, sl st in ch st between next 2 petals) 5 times, ch 3; join with sl st in same st as beg sl st. (6 ch-3 sps)

Rnd 4: Ch 1, turn, * (sc, hdc, 3 dc, hdc, sc) in next ch-3 sp, rep from * around; join with sl st in beg sc. (6 petals)

Rnd 5: Ch 1, turn, (working behind Rnd 4) sl st in same st as joining sl st, * (ch 4, sl st in ch st between next 2 petals) 5 times, ch 4; join with sl st in same st as beg sl st. (6 ch-4 sps)

Rnd 6: Ch 1, turn, * (sc, hdc, 3 dc, hdc, sc) in next ch-4 sp, rep from * around; join with sl st in beg sc. (6 petals)

Fasten off. Weave in ends.

Coral Reef Blooms

These multi-petal blooms look as if they can be found in the coral reefs fifty leagues under the sea. Transform your little one into your own little mermaid by putting one on her hat or hair treasure! These flowers can be made smaller or larger by increasing or decreasing the number of chains for the petals. Make it a single-tiered bloom or try making each tier a different color.

MATERIALS

Light sport weight yarn 🧶 3
in the color of your choice

Size I (5.5mm) crochet hook

Tapestry needle

Scissors

Finished Project Size

Approx. 4" × 1" (10.2cm × 2.5cm) across

Gauge

No gauge required.

> This flower is worked in two continuous rounds, first working in the front loops, then working in the back loops. For a refresher on working in the front loops (flps) and back loops (blps), see Techniques & Stitches.

Glossary of Abbreviations

ch(s)	chain(s)
st(s)	stitch(es)
sl st	slip stitch
beg	beginning
rep	repeat
flp(s)	front loop(s)
blp(s)	back loop(s)
sc	single crochet
hdc	half double crochet
*	repeat instructions following the asterisk as directed
( )	work instructions within the parenthesis as many times as directed

Make the Coral Reef Blooms

Ch 5; join with sl st in beg ch to form ring.

Rnd 1: Ch 1, work 10 sc in ring, join with sl st in flp (do not sl st through both loops). (10 sc)

Rnd 2: Working in flps, ch 8, hdc in 2nd ch from hook and in next 6 chs, sl st in same flp st as joining sl st (petal made), * (sl st, ch 8, hdc in 2nd ch from hook and in next 6 chs, sl st) in next flp, rep from * around, working one petal in each sc (do not join). (10 petals)

Rnd 3: Working in blps, * (sl st, ch 8, hdc in 2nd ch from hook and in next 6 chs, sl st) in next blp, rep from * around, working one petal in each sc; join with sl st in beg sl st. (10 petals).

Fasten off. Weave in ends.

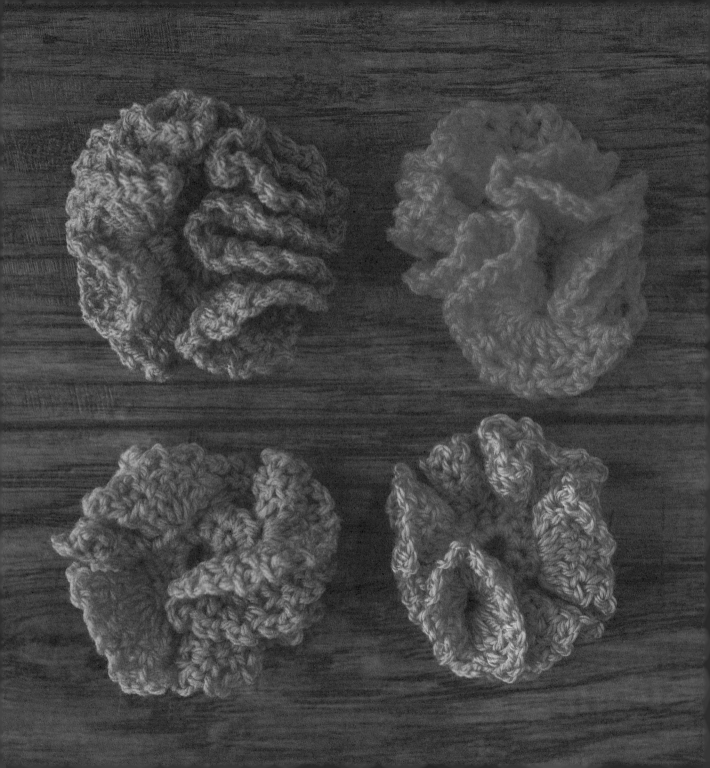

Carnation Puffs

These big Carnation Puffs remind me of fluffy clouds or cotton balls. Don't be afraid to experiment by using textured yarns to make them. Each one will have a different look than the next. Use them in place of bows on gifts, or use cotton yarn to create soft, luxurious bath puffs or eco-friendly dish scrubbies—perfect for those nonstick pots and pans that need extra-special care.

MATERIALS

Light sport weight yarn [3] in the color of your choice

Size I (5.5mm) crochet hook

Tapestry needle

Scissors

Finished Project Size

Approx. 4½" × 1½" (11.4cm × 3.8cm) across

Gauge

No gauge required.

Glossary of Abbreviations

ch(s)	chain(s)
st(s)	stitch(s)
sl st	slip stitch
beg	beginning
sk	skip
rep	repeat
sc	single crochet
hdc	half double crochet
dc	double crochet
*	repeat instructions following the asterisk as directed

Make the Carnation Puffs

Ch 5; join with sl st in beg ch to form ring.

Rnd 1: Ch 1, work 11 sc in ring; join with sl st in beg sc. (11 sc)

Rnd 2: Ch 2, hdc in same st as joining, * 2 hdc in next sc, rep from * around; join with sl st in 2nd ch of beg ch-2. (22 hdc)

Rnd 3: Ch 3, 4 dc in same st as joining, * 5 dc in next hdc, rep from * around; join with sl st in 3rd ch of beg ch-3. (110 dc)

Rnd 4: Ch 1, sc in same st as joining, * ch 2, sc in next dc, ch 3, sk next dc, sc in next dc, rep from * around to last st, ch 2, sc in last st, ch 3, join with sl st in beg sc. (74 ch sps)

Fasten off. Weave in ends.

Pinwheel Posies

Plant an entire garden on the side of your hat using these airy posies. Sew them onto a dress or handbag, or decorate a sweet baby blanket to make it a beautiful heirloom keepsake. Attach them to pens for colorful desk accessories.

MATERIALS

Light sport weight yarn in the color of your choice

Size I (5.5mm) crochet hook

Tapestry needle

Scissors

Finished Project Size

Approx. 3½" (8.9cm) wide

Gauge

No gauge required.

Glossary of Abbreviations

ch(s)	chain(s)
st(s)	stitch(s)
sl st	slip stitch
sp(s)	space(s)
beg	beginning
rep	repeat
rnd	round
sc	single crochet
hdc	half double crochet
*	repeat instructions following the asterisk as directed
( )	work instructions within the parentheses as many times as directed

Make the Pinwheel Posies

Ch 5; join with sl st in beg ch to form ring.

Rnd 1: Ch 1, sc in ring, (ch 6, sc in ring, ch 7, sc in ring) 2 times, ch 6, sc in ring, ch 7; join with sl st in beg sc. (6 ch sps)

Rnd 2: Do not chain; * 7 hdc in ch-6 sp, sl st in sc, 8 hdc in ch-7 sp, sl st in sc, rep from * around; join with sl st to Rnd 1 sc. (45 hdc)

Fasten off. Weave in ends.

Cherry Blossoms

There are so many possibilities for these blossoms. I see them draped from corner to corner, hanging on a crocheted chain to make an adorable garland or dangling off a ribbon on a one-of-a-kind baby mobile. I even see them draped on a curtain rod in the kitchen, each one made in a bright color. How cute would these be made out of a finer yarn and added to the end of a few bobby pins? Sew a button onto a hair elastic and interchange them to match your wardrobe. Your friends will adore your embellished necklace or bracelet featuring these cherry blossoms. You control how small or how big you make them by using different thicknesses of yarns and sizes of hooks.

MATERIALS

Light sport weight yarn **3** in the color of your choice

Size I (5.5mm) crochet hook

Tapestry needle

Scissors

Finished Project Size

Small: Approx. 3" (7.6cm) across

Regular: Approx. 3½"(8.9cm) across

Gauge

No gauge required.

Glossary of Abbreviations

ch(s)	chain(s)
st(s)	stitch(s)
sl st	slip stitch
sp(s)	space(s)
beg	beginning
sk	skip
rep	repeat
rnd	round
sc	single crochet
dc	double crochet
tc	treble crochet
*	repeat instructions following the asterisk as directed
( )	work instructions within the parentheses as many times as directed

Make the Cherry Blossoms (Small)

Ch 5. Join with sl st in beg ch to form ring.

Rnd 1: Ch 1, work 9 sc in ring, join with sl st in beg sc. (9 sc)

Rnd 2: Ch 1, sc in same st as joining, (ch 2, sk next sc, sc in next sc) 4 times, ch 2; join with sl st in beg sc. (5 ch-2 sps)

Rnd 3: Do not chain, * (sl st, ch 2, 4 dc, ch 2, sl st) in next ch-2 sp, rep from * around; join with sl st in beg sl st. (5 petals)

Fasten off. Weave in ends.

Make the Cherry Blossoms (Regular)

Ch 5. Join with sl st in beg ch to form ring.

Rnd 1: Ch 1, work 9 sc in ring, join with sl st in beg sc. (9 sc)

Rnd 2: Ch 1, sc in same st as joining, (ch 2, sk next sc, sc in next sc) 4 times, ch 2; join with sl st in beg sc. (5 ch-2 sps)

Rnd 3: Do not chain, * (sl st, ch 3, 4 tc, ch 3, sl st) in next ch-2 sp, rep from * around; join with sl st in beg sl st. (5 petals)

Fasten off. Weave in ends.

What a Great Idea

Blossom Bobby Pins

These simple and elegant bobby pins make a great addition to your hair accessories collection. I used a thinner cotton yarn and a smaller hook to create the flowers, then tied them onto a bobby pin. Attach these flowers to any kind of hair clip or fabric headband to create a great hair accessory, and don't be afraid to experiment with textured yarns.

Gorgeous Garland

This garland would look great draped over kitchen curtains, in a baby's room or made in Christmas colors to decorate a Christmas tree. All you need to do is chain away! To create this easy garland, chain the length you need and fasten off. Next, crochet the cherry blossoms in the colors of your choice. Cut one piece of yarn approximately 8" (20.3cm) long for each blossom you make. You will use these strands to attach the blossoms to the chain. Pull the yarn through the blossom petal and the chain, then back through the chain and blossom petal again and tie it in a bow. Make sure the flowers are evenly spaced on the chain. This is a quick and easy way to brighten any room.

Blossom Baby Mobile

How sweet would one of these mobiles be hanging in a baby's room? To make a mobile, you need a grapevine wreath, ribbon, a tapestry needle, yarn, buttons and some Cherry Blossoms. First, using two strands of yarn, crochet two long chains. (The length of the chain depends on how far down from the ceiling you want it to hang. These chains will attach from one side to the other side of the wreath, alternating sides.) Once you have chained the desired length, turn and hdc in the 2nd ch from the hook. Proceed to hdc in each remaining chain. Sew or tie the hdc chain ends to the wreath using the picture for placement. Gather the middles and tie into a knot. Next, cut the ribbon into the desired lengths and sew them onto the wreath, making sure they are evenly spaced. Sew buttons onto the tops and bottoms of the ribbon. Make the blossoms in the colors of your choice and place them onto the buttons. Now you have a one-of-a-kind baby mobile!

Swirl Flowers

I simply adore the curves of this flower; it has such a beautiful, unique look. Create your Swirl Flowers by using different textures and thicknesses of yarns. Each one will look like a little masterpiece!

MATERIALS

Light sport weight yarn **(3)** in two colors of your choice

Size I (5.5mm) crochet hook

Tapestry needle

Scissors

Finished Project Size

Small: Approx. 3" (7.6cm) across

Regular: Approx. 4" (10.2cm) across

Gauge

No gauge required.

Glossary of Abbreviations

ch(s)	chain(s)
st(s)	stitch(s)
sl st	slip stitch
sp(s)	space(s)
beg	beginning
rep	repeat
rnd	round
sc	single crochet
hdc	half double crochet
*	repeat instructions following the asterisk as directed
( )	work instructions within parentheses as many times as directed

Make the Small Swirl Flower (5 Petals)

With main flower color, ch 5; join with sl st in beg ch to form ring.

Rnd 1: (Ch 5, sl st in ring) 5 times. (5 ch-5 loops)

Rnd 2: Do not join; * 9 hdc in next ch-5 loop, work 2 hdc in the center ring over the sl st from Rnd 1, rep from * around; join trim color with sl st in beg hdc. (55 hdc)

Rnd 3: Ch 1, sc in same st as joining and in each hdc around; join with sl st in beg sc. (55 sc)

Fasten off. Weave in ends. Form the flower into shape with your fingers.

Make the Regular Swirl Flower (6 Petals)

With main flower color, ch 5; join with sl st in beg ch to form ring.

Rnd 1: (Ch 8, sl st in ring) 6 times. (6 ch-8 loops)

Rnd 2: Do not join; * 12 hdc in next ch-8 loop, work 2 hdc in the center ring over the sl st from Rnd 1, rep from * around, join trim color with sl st in beg hdc. (84 hdc)

Rnd 3: Ch 1, sc in same st as joining and in each hdc around; join with sl st in beg sc. (84 sc)

Fasten off. Weave in ends. Form the flower into shape with your fingers.

Flopsy Hares

Here comes Peter Cottontail, hopping down the bunny trail. . . . These bunny rabbit motifs are perfect for decorating children's Easter baskets before they go looking for their eggs. Button one on her new headband, or add it to a hairclip to match her beautiful Easter dress. Perhaps you know of a little cherub who loves bath-time toys. Crochet a few of these in 100% cotton yarn and tub time will become an instant hit!

MATERIALS

Light sport weight yarn
in the color of your choice

Size I (5.5mm) crochet hook

Tapestry needle

Scissors

Finished Project Size

2¾" × 3" (6.7cm × 7.6cm)

Gauge

No gauge required.

Glossary of Abbreviations

ch(s)	chain(s)
st(s)	stitch(s)
sl st	slip stitch
beg	beginning
sk	skip
rep	repeat
rnd	round
prev	previous
hdc	half double crochet
dc	double crochet
*	repeat instructions following the asterisk as directed

Make the Flopsy Hares

Ch 5; join with sl st in beg ch to form ring.

Rnd 1: Ch 3, work 13 dc in ring, join with sl st in 3rd ch of beg ch-3. (14 dc)

Rnd 2: Ch 2, hdc in same st as joining, * 2 hdc in next dc, rep from * around, join with sl st in 2nd ch of beg ch-2. (28 hdc)

Rnd 3: Ch 1, sk next hdc, sl st in next hdc, ch 14, sl st in prev sk hdc, sl st in next unworked hdc (in the hdc after ch-14 st), sl st in next 3 hdc, sk next hdc, sl st in next hdc, ch 14, sl st in prev sk hdc, sl st in next unworked hdc (in the hdc after ch 14-st), * sl st in next 19 hdc; join with sl st in beg ch-1. (28 sl st)

Fasten off. Weave in ends.

Make the Bow

To finish, tie a small piece of yarn or ribbon in the color of your choice to the base of the ear or neck and tie in a bow. Trim the ends if desired.

What a Great Idea

Custom Easter Baskets

Who wouldn't love waking up Easter morning to find a herd of these little bunnies gathered on his or her Easter basket? To create these custom baskets, sew several ⅞"–1" (2.2cm–2.5cm) buttons on the basket where you would like the bunnies placed (leave the yarn ends facing outward. These will be the whiskers). Simply button the bunnies onto the buttons and unravel the yarn ends to create their whiskers! It's a quick and easy transformation for a plain basket.

Cotton Tub Toys

By making the motifs out of 100% cotton yarn, you can create adorable little toys for your kids to play with in the bathtub! These would also make great wipes for babies because they're soft on the skin.

Sweet Hearts

In just two rounds, you can create these adorable Sweet Hearts. They're easy to make and beautiful to look at. Add one to your handmade Valentine's Day card to give it a more personal touch, or sew two together (back to back) in different colors and hang them in the baby's room above the crib or over the chair. As you rock your baby, they can see and feel the love in the air.

MATERIALS

Light sport weight yarn in the color of your choice

Size I (5.5mm) crochet hook

Tapestry needle

Scissors

Finished Project Size
3½" × 3" (8.9cm × 7.6cm)

Gauge
No gauge required.

> When you begin making the heart, you will be working up toward the top left arc, then around.

Glossary of Abbreviations

ch(s)	chain(s)
st(s)	stitch
sl st	slip stitch
beg	beginning
rnd	round
sc	single crochet
hdc	half double crochet
dc	double crochet
tc	treble crochet
picot st	picot stitch
( )	work instructions within the parentheses as many times as directed

Make the Sweet Hearts

Ch 5; join with sl st in beg ch to form ring.

Rnd 1: Ch 1, (sc, hdc, dc, 3 tc, 5 dc, picot st, 5 dc, 3 tc, dc, hdc, sc) in center ring; join with sl st in beg sc. (22 sts)

Rnd 2: Do not chain; sc in next hdc, hdc in next dc, 2 hdc in 1st tc, 3 hdc in 2nd tc, 2 hdc in 3rd tc, hdc in next 5 dc, hdc in 1st ch of picot st, 3 hdc in 2nd ch of picot st, hdc in 3rd ch of picot st, hdc in next 5 dc, 2 hdc in next tc, 3 hdc in 2nd tc, 2 hdc in last tc, hdc in next dc, sc in last hdc st; join with sl st in beg sc. (33 sts)

Fasten off. Weave in ends.

What a Great Idea

Make your Sweet Hearts even sweeter by creating a slip stitch border in a different color yarn.

After creating a Sweet Heart using the basic pattern, follow the steps below:

1. Using trim color (TC) of your choice, insert hook through any hdc st around the last rnd of the heart.

2. Draw yarn up through st (*diag 1*).

3. Insert hook into next hdc and sl st. Proceed to sl st in each st around outside of the entire heart to the last st (*diag 2*).

4. When you reach the last st, drop the loop off your hook and place hook under the heart. Insert hook from bottom up into center of first sl st made. Use fingers to place loop over hook and draw it down through center of 1st sl st.

5. Cut yarn and pull end through loop. Pull tight, tie both ends together and weave in ends.

Sweet Heart with Slip Stitch Edge (*diag. 1*)

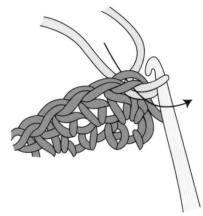

Sweet Heart with Slip Stitch Edge (*diag. 2*)

All-Season Wreath

What an easy way to decorate your room or front door! All you need is a grapevine wreath, ribbon, buttons and some Sweet Hearts. This is a great way to display those vintage buttons you've been saving for a special project.

First, wrap the ribbon around the wreath. (If you use wired ribbon, you can twist it around a piece of the wreath to start it and end it, and it will stay in place.) Next, sew ⅞"–1" (2.2cm–2.5cm) buttons onto the wreath where you would like the Sweet Hearts to go (leaving the yarn ends facing outward will give the wreath a unique look). Lastly, make some Sweet Hearts in the colors of your choice. Button the hearts onto the wreath and voila! You have a great addition to your home.

These wreaths are perfect for celebrating any occasion. Just change the ribbons, colors and motifs to make a great piece for any season or holiday. White, pink and red hearts are perfect for Valentine's Day, while bunnies are great for Easter. White, red and green Carnation Puffs are lovely for Christmas. The possibilities are endless.

Bear Hugs

Bear Hugs are so simple to make and so much fun to play with! For a quick baby shower gift, make them using cotton yarn, and they magically turn into baby bath wipes. While you're at it, make some face scrubbies for yourself, and your children will love having a few as toys for the bathtub.

MATERIALS

Light sport weight yarn in the color of your choice

Size I (5.5mm) crochet hook

Tapestry needle

Scissors

Finished Project Size

2¾" × 3" (6.7cm × 7.6cm)

Gauge

No gauge required.

Glossary of Abbreviations

ch(s)	chain(s)
st(s)	stitch(s)
sl st	slip stitch
beg	beginning
sk	skip
rep	repeat
rnd	round
hdc	half double crochet
dc	double crochet
*	repeat instructions following the asterisk as directed

Make each bear unique by sewing facial features on them. Try cutting out felt to make a tiny bow tie for a boy bear or adding rosy cheeks or a tiny flower to a girl bear's ear.

Make the Bear Hugs

Ch 5; join with sl st in beg ch to form ring.

Rnd 1: Ch 3, work 13 dc in ring; join with sl st in 3rd ch of beg ch-3. (14 dc)

Rnd 2: Ch 2, hdc in same st as joining, * 2 hdc in next dc, rep from * around; join with sl st in 2nd ch of beg ch-2. (28 hdc)

Rnd 3: Do not chain, sl st in next hdc, sk next hdc, 8 dc in next hdc, sk next hdc, sl st in next 4 hdc, sk next hdc, 8 dc in next hdc, sk next hdc, sl st in next 17 hdc, then join with sl st in the beg sl st. (16 dc, 22 sl sts)

Fasten off. Weave in ends.

Butterfly Kisses

These adorable butterflies make me think of fairies, free to fly anywhere they choose. Wouldn't they make the perfect finishing touch for a fairy wand? Just attach one to the end of the wand and add long pieces of yarn or ribbon for the tail, and you have a unique wand for your little princess. Or how about embellishing purses and giving them as gifts? The possibilities are endless!

MATERIALS

Light sport weight yarn  in the color of your choice for the butterfly

Light sport weight yarn in the color of your choice for the antennae

Size I (5.5mm) crochet hook

Tapestry needle

Scissors

Finished Project Size

2¾" × 3" (6.7cm × 7.6cm)

Gauge

No gauge required.

Glossary of Abbreviations

ch(s)	chain(s)
st(s)	stitch(s)
sl st	slip stitch
sp(s)	space(s)
beg	beginning
rep	repeat
rnd	round
sc	single crochet
hdc	half double crochet
dc	double crochet
tc	treble crochet
sl st	slip stitch
( )	work instructions within the parentheses as many times as directed

Make the Butterfly Kisses

Ch 5; join with sl st in beg ch to form ring.

Rnd 1: Ch 1, sc in ring, (ch 3, sc in ring) 3 times, ch 3; join with sl st in beg sc. (4 ch-3 sp)

Rnd 2: Ch 1, sl st in 2nd ch of next ch-3 sp, ch 4, (tc, 3 dc, hdc) in same ch-3 sp, sl st in sc, (8 dc in next ch-3 sp, sl st in sc) 2 times, (hdc, 3 dc, tc) in last ch-3 sp, ch 4, sl st in 2nd ch of the same ch-3 sp, ch 1, join with sl st in beg ch-1. (28 sts)

Fasten off. Weave in ends.

Make the Antennae

Ch 14 and fasten off.

To Attach the Antennae

Turn the butterfly over (wrong-side up) and insert the hook in the middle ring. Fold the antennae in half, placing the middle of the antennae over the hook, and pull the middle antennae loop through the ring of the butterfly. Holding the ends in the opposite hand, bring the hook up and over between the 2 pointed wings. Fold the antennae ends over the hook and pull the antennae ends through the middle of the antennae loop. Pull tight and trim the ends of the antennae if desired.

Index

Dedication

This book is dedicated to my husband, Kurtis. Not once have you complained about my obsession with crocheting and yarn. When I crochet from morning to the wee hours of the next morning, you have let me be, letting me enjoy my passion. I love you forever and always.

And to my two boys, Campbell and Tait: I love you with all my heart. Thank you for being so patient while I was writing my book. You are such amazing boys, each of you unique in your own way. I am truly blessed. I love you both to infinity times a kazillion!

About the Author

Shauna-Lee Graham resides on a farm in Innisfil, Ontario, Canada, with her husband, Kurtis, their two boys, Campbell and Tait, and their two dogs, Charlee and Daisy. She has been an avid crocheter since she was young. She started her home-based crochet business in 2009.

Visit the author's website at www.bouquetbeanies.com and her Facebook page at www.facebook.com/BouquetBeanies.

Acknowledgments

I could not have completed this book without the support and encouragement of so many people.

To my mom, Kathy Gates. Thank you for having the patience to teach me to crochet so many years ago. Who would have thought that crocheting would turn into my passion. I am so thankful to have you as my mom, always there for me, no matter what. I love you!

To my brother, Tim Fitchett, and his wife, Kim (who is truly the sister I never had), who encouraged and believed in me right from the beginning of this adventure!

To Linda and Murray Graham, the best in-laws ever. Thank you so much for all your encouragement and support, not only while I was writing this book, but every day!

To my great friends Dee-Anne Benson and Lorie Merritt, who are always there for me, through thick and thin, never doubting for a minute that I could do this!

To Julie Gillies, who became the most amazing friend to me during and after this journey. I can't thank you enough for all your help, which seemed like ages of testing patterns over and over again. You were always happy to help me, and you are such a beautiful person—you rock!

To all my pattern testers who have helped me along the way: Julie Gillies, Dee-Anne Benson, Angela Geist, Patty Quirk, Marta Traylor, Moira Richardson, Jamie Triplett, Tessa Rasnick, Susan Pokrak Chan, Lou Dale, Cathy Ypma, Gayle Patriquen, Peggy Savory and to all the others who took the time out of their busy schedules to help me test my creations. I am truly grateful.

To Nicole Snow at darngoodyarn.com. What can I say? You have been an inspiration to me, with your encouragement, help, guidance and beautiful yarns. You have been an absolute godsend, helping me through this journey. Thank you so much, my friend!

To Amelia Johanson, acquisitions editor at F+W Media, who emailed me out of the blue one day with a book proposition. Thank you for taking a chance on turning this crocheter into a first-time author and giving me the opportunity to shine!

To Noel Rivera, my editor at F+W Media, for all your hard work and guiding me every step of the way. I simply could not have done this without you!

To Corrie Schaffeld and his family for some truly beautiful photography.

To all the behind-the-scenes staff at F+W Media, a huge thank you for all your hard work in bringing this book to life!

A special thank you to Adria at Inspired Images Photography and Shelly Pilote and Cindy Desbien for your amazing talents in getting me ready for my photo.

And to my husband, Kurtis, and our two boys. Thank you for waiting so patiently for this book to be finished.

fw media

www.fwmedia.com

18 17 16 15 14   5 4 3 2 1

DISTRIBUTED IN CANADA BY FRASER DIRECT
100 Armstrong Avenue
Georgetown, ON, Canada L7G 5S4
Tel: (905) 877-4411

DISTRIBUTED IN THE U.K. AND EUROPE BY F+W MEDIA
INTERNATIONAL
Brunel House, Newton Abbot, Devon, TQ12 4PU, England
Tel: (+44) 1626 323200   Fax: (+44) 1626 323319
E-mail: postmaster@davidandcharles.co.uk

DISTRIBUTED IN AUSTRALIA BY CAPRICORN LINK
P.O. Box 704, S. Windsor NSW, 2756 Australia
Tel: (02) 4560-1600   Fax: (02) 4577-5288
E-mail: books@capricornlink.com.au

ISBN: 978-1-4402-3755-3
SRN: U5659

Editor: Noel Rivera
Book designer & photographer: Corrie Schaffeld of 1326 Studios
Author photographer: Adria Frappier of Inspired Images
Production coordinator: Greg Nock

Metric Conversion Chart

To convert	to	multiply by
Inches	Centimeters	2.54
Centimeters	Inches	0.4
Feet	Centimeters	30.5
Centimeters	Feet	0.03
Yards	Meters	0.9
Meters	Yards	1.1

More fun with color and yarn!

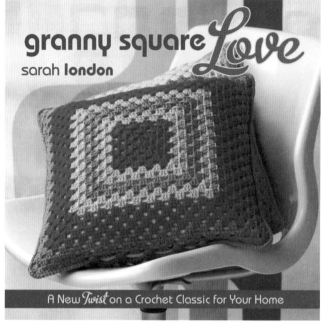

Knit and felt your own cute collection of kittens, garden of cacti or assortment of robots with these 16 adorable amigurumi designs, perfect for making and sharing. These *kawaii*-inspired projects are knitted with worsted weight, 100% wool yarn, and handfelted for a super-cute, solid finish.

ISBN: 978-1-4402-3576-4
SRN: U3143

The granny square is a classic crochet motif that has graced innumerable afghans. In *Granny Square Love*, author Sarah London breathes new life into this tried-and-true favorite by taking this motif out of the afghan so you can use it throughout your home or make quick gifts for any occasion.

ISBN: 978-1-4403-1294-6
SRN: W0657

Check out crochetme.com for more fantastic crochet creations!